The Expert Witness, Forensic Science and the Criminal Justice Systems of the UK

The Expert Witness, Forensic Science and the Criminal Justice Systems of the UK

Edited by
Lucina Hackman, Fiona Raitt and Sue Black

CRC Press
Taylor & Francis Group
Boca Raton London New York

CRC Press is an imprint of the
Taylor & Francis Group, an **informa** business

CRC Press
Taylor & Francis Group
6000 Broken Sound Parkway NW, Suite 300
Boca Raton, FL 33487-2742

Printed on acid-free paper

International Standard Book Number-13: 978-1-4987-0569-1 (Paperback)

Visit the Taylor & Francis Web site at
http://www.taylorandfrancis.com

and the CRC Press Web site at
http://www.crcpress.com

Contents

Preface

The role of the expert witness and the opinion evidence that they present in court has caused, and continues to cause, issues; experts often do not agree and may hold widely differing opinions or may present their evidence in ways which make it difficult for a jury to follow. More recently, the increase in the use of DNA evidence to examine past cases has shown that experts can be the cause of miscarriages of justice. It quickly becomes apparent that the issues around the use of expert witnesses are global, but each criminal justice system has differences that anyone attending court in this role needs to understand prior to giving evidence. Despite this, the literature which exists around the role of the expert is surprisingly limited in scope.

The idea for this book came about from a series of conversations between ourselves as we tried to find information in the literature about the role of the expert witness in the courts of Scotland. As we looked around, we found that information we needed was not readily available and so we decided to address the gaps through this book. It was during the writing of this book that Professor Raitt retired from her position as professor of evidence and social justice at the Law School at Dundee University. During her time at Dundee, she cast a close look at the role of expert scientific evidence in Scottish courts, detailing the role that this has played in cases across the country.

Chapter 1 studies the ethical obligations of the expert witness, exploring the ongoing discursive around the ethical obligations of the expert and how these should be fulfilled within their role as the expert, taking into account existing legislation. Within this narrative is an emphasis on the importance of ethics in gaining the trust of those listening to the opinion of the expert within the court, including the members of the jury.

Chapters 2 and 3 both look at the development of the role of the expert witness in relation to case law, inquiries and miscarriages of justice. The law is constantly developing and responding, and these chapters trace and discuss how these changes have impacted the modern role of the expert witness.

Much of the discussion that sits around the role of the expert witness concentrates on the expert as prosecution witness. However, Chapter 4 takes a look at the role of the expert as a defence witness within the Scottish legal system. The chapter highlights some of the differences of the Scottish system but also includes experiences that the author has gained from working within this system. This leads to Chapter 5, which offers a similar discussion of the role of the expert witness within the legal system of Northern Ireland, and where this differs from the jurisdictions of England, Wales and Scotland.

Chapter 6 outlines the responsibilities and obligations of the expert in relation to present legislation, leading to Chapter 7, which looks at the difficult subject of expert evidence and emerging sciences. The way in which the court and the expert deal with these new evidence types is important, and each presents its own challenges, not least of which are the ways in which the varying professional groups within the legal system wish to use this emerging science, and the stresses and pressures that this imposes on the system and the expert witness themselves. Chapter 8 follows logically on from this as it examines the relationship between expert evidence and statistics. The way in which statistics is utilised and presented has come under increasing scrutiny by the courts, and this chapter discusses the difficulties that exist for both sides in this debate.

Finally, Chapters 9 and 10 add an international perspective. Many experts will find themselves working across jurisdictions, so an understanding of how this impacts their role within the court system is vital. Chapter 9 compares the role of the expert witness in inquisitorial systems with the role of the expert in adversarial systems; and Chapter 10 rounds this off with an examination of the way in which the U.S. Supreme Court's decision in *Melendez-Diaz* in 2009 impacted the role of the expert witness.

As with any book of this type, this required the work of a number of people. The editors are grateful to all the contributors, but special mention should go to Dr David Lucy, who contributed a chapter to this book but sadly lost his battle against cancer in June 2018. David started his career in Edinburgh before working for a number of years at the Joseph Bell Centre for Forensic Statistics and Legal Reasoning. From there he moved to Lancaster University. His publications and work on statistics for the analysis and understanding of forensic evidence brought the subject of statistics within the understanding of many students.

Dr Lucina Hackman
Prof Fiona Raitt
Prof Dame Sue Black

Acknowledgements

The editors would like to thank all of the contributors to this book for their assistance in the production of this text. We are also grateful to the editorial and production teams at the publishers, particularly to Mark Listewnik for his patience and the time taken to keep us on the right path.

Editors

Dr Lucina Hackman is currently a principal investigator in education and training in forensic science at the Leverhulme Research Centre for Forensic Science and the University of Dundee. Prior to this she was a senior lecturer at the Centre for Anatomy and Human Identification, where she was responsible for MSc courses. She is the co-editor of two books on human identification and has authored book chapters in the same area. She is chair of the Forensic Anthropology Steering Committee at the Royal Anthropological Institute, and was lead author in writing the discipline Code of Practice. She is a fellow of the Royal Anthropological Institute and the Royal Society of Biology and a level 1 certified forensic anthropologist.

Prof Fiona Raitt, LLB, PhD, co-founded Wilson & Raitt, a Dundee-based firm of solicitors, where she has worked as a solicitor for 13 years, often representing survivors of domestic abuse.

Until her recent retirement, she was professor of evidence and social justice at the University of Dundee, where she undertook research in the areas of evidence law, domestic abuse, sexual violence and family law.

Her books include *Laws of Evidence in Scotland* and *Evidence: Principles, Policy and Practice* (2008, revised edition in 2013) and, with Dr Suzanne Zeedyk, *The Implicit Relation of Psychology and Law: Women and Syndrome Evidence* (2002).

Prof Dame Sue Black is pro vice chancellor for engagement at Lancaster University. Prior to this appointment she was director of the Leverhulme Research Centre for Forensic Science and director of the Centre for Anatomy and Human Identification, both at the University of Dundee. She is the president of the Royal Anthropological Institute, patron of archaeology in Scotland and the lifetime professor of anatomy at the Royal Scottish Academy. She is the author of 15 textbooks in the fields of human anatomy and forensic anthropology, and has given expert evidence in courts throughout the UK and overseas. In 2001, she was awarded an Order of the British Empire (OBE) for leading forensic anthropology in the British Forensic Team in Kosovo, and in 2016 she was awarded a DBE (Dame Commander) to recognise her leadership in forensic science. She is a fellow of the Royal Society of Edinburgh, the Royal Anthropological Institute, the Royal Society of Biology and the Royal College of Physicians of Edinburgh; and is a level 1 certified forensic anthropologist.

Contributors

Prof Jonathan Doak is professor of criminal justice and associate dean for research at Nottingham Law School, Nottingham Trent University. His research focuses on issues relating to the rights of victims, defendants and witnesses within the criminal trial; and wider issues relating to criminal procedure (particularly criminal evidence, cross-examination and restorative justice) and transitional justice (particularly in relation to process and reparation).

Tim Jebb, married with two children, was called to the bar of Northern Ireland in 2012. He previously worked as a solicitor specialising in criminal law. In his time at the bar, he has continued to practice in this area, and also now accepts instructions in the field of immigration law and judicial review.

Eamon P. H. Keane is a Scottish solicitor and legal author with a special interest in the law of evidence and the prosecution of sexual offences. He is the co-editor of *Raitt on Evidence: Principles, Policy and Practice.* He is the convenor of the Scottish Legal Action Group. He has practiced as a criminal defence solicitor and currently works at the Scottish Criminal Cases Review Commission.

Dr David Lucy worked at the University of Lancaster as a lecturer. He specialised in the application of statistical methods to the evaluation of forensic evidence, about which he published widely.

Prof Verena Murschetz is a professor of law at the Criminal Law Department at the University of Innsbruck in Austria. In 2015, she was appointed as the chair of the Expert Commission 1 of the Austrian Ombudsman Board, acting as the National Preventive Mechanism under the Optional Protocol to the Convention against Torture (OPCAT) for a 6-year mandate. Prof Murschetz has published extensively in the fields of criminal law and criminal procedure, as well as European and international criminal law. Her publications have received numerous awards, such as the *Otto Seibert Wissenschaftspreis*, the *Franz Gschnitzer Preis* and the *Preis des Akademischen Alpinen Vereins.* After completing her law studies at the University of Innsbruck, she obtained an LLM from the University of California at Los Angeles and a PhD summa cum laude as well as her habilitation from the University of Innsbruck.

Between 2003 and 2010, she regularly taught courses on international criminal law and European Union law at the Victoria University of Wellington School of Law.

Prof Niamh Nic Daéid is a professor of forensic science and director of the Leverhulme Research Centre for Forensic Science, a 10-year, £10-million research centre focusing on positively disrupting the forensic science ecosystem. She undertakes forensic casework mainly in fire investigation and drug analysis, and has provided evidence to the criminal courts and public inquiry as an expert witness.

Prof Jessica Smith, W. R. Kenan, Jr. distinguished professor of public law and government, is a faculty member at the School of Government, University of North Carolina at Chapel Hill. Prof Smith teaches judges and other public officials about criminal law and evidence, and works on projects to create a fairer and more effective criminal justice system. She received the Friend of the Court Award from the North Carolina Supreme Court for her role in a 2017 law that reformed the state's juvenile justice system; she currently is working on projects regarding overcriminalization and bail reform.

Prof Tony Ward is professor of law at Northumbria University, Newcastle. He has published several articles and book chapters on forensic science evidence, including a contribution to *Forensic Science Evidence and Expert Witness Testimony: Reliability through Reform?* edited by Paul Roberts and Michael Stockdale (Edward Elgar, 2018). Other recent publications include *State Crime and Civil Activism* with Penny Green (Routledge, 2018).

Sheriff Tom Welsh QC was appointed sheriff in 2000. He was director of the Judicial Institute for Scotland for 5 years and presently sits in Edinburgh Sheriff Court.

Introduction

The role of the expert has a long history in UK courts and remains the primary method by which scientific evidence is introduced into the courtroom. This has meant that the role of the expert witness has remained an important role within the presentation of a case. The expert witness is by definition an individual who has experience, knowledge and expertise in a defined area and is within the courtroom to communicate their independent opinion on evidence that has been recovered and, through doing so, assist the court to reach a final decision on the facts of the case before it. The expert is alone in their ability to present their opinion to the courtroom and, as defined in legislation, must be '*objective and unbiased*'[1] and give an opinion that is '*within their area of expertise*'.[2] In the UK, the duty is to the court, rather than to whoever has paid for their work, and therefore the court is their ultimate end user. While their work might be utilised during the investigation, it is within the courtroom where their work must be presented and judged. Given the importance of this, it is surprising how little comprehensive guidance there is in relation to their role. For those starting in this role, the guidance[3] and existing legislation[4] that do exist have to be pieced together to try and form a coherent guide to their actions. This book tries to fill some of that gap for both those who are entering into the role of an expert witness but also for those who utilise the services of an expert within the courtroom.

While the role of the expert does have a long history, those undertaking it have to adapt and change with legislation and case law. The change in immunity of the expert is a good example of this. For over 400 years, an individual who was acting in the role of an expert witness for the UK courts had immunity;[5] however, in a move that reflected the changing role of the expert to that of independent scientists who were re-numerated for their work, this immunity was removed in 2011.[6] The expert's central role is to give opinion evidence to the court, and this is reflected in the discussion made by the judges in *Jones v Kaney*,[7] where the potential for this ruling to limit the number of people who are willing to undertake the role of an expert was discussed. The judges stated that since the expert has a duty to the court, they would not be at risk as long as they inform the court if they do have a change of opinion and if they ensure that they fulfil their responsibilities in relation to the court. Indeed it was mooted that this decision would ensure that experts are more circumspect about their evidence and ensure that it is accurate when presenting to the court.

Complicated scientific and other evidence which may be central to questions of identity, for example, is introduced to the court by expert witnesses, demonstrating the importance of the role. The complexity of the evidence does not just relate to interpretation of that evidence but the way in which it is communicated. Poor communication can leave those listening at best confused and at worst with a misapprehension about the meaning or weight of the evidence placed before them. The ability to communicate complicated scientific evidence in a way that is accessible to judges and juries is, however, only part of the role of the expert. The expert must also ensure that they adhere to the duties and requirements associated with their role. They must record in detail all of the work that they undertake, they must retain all material that they produce and they must ensure that when asked all records are made available to the defence. While the actions that are required of experts are set out in these guidances, and indeed, in England and Wales, any report must now be accompanied by a statement that these have been complied with, it has often been the case that failure to follow these have resulted in high-profile miscarriages of justice. Each case of this type provides important lessons for the expert, with a number of themes arising regularly throughout; however, it is clear that these are not always communicated to experts about to embark on their new role within the legal system.

As scientific tests become more sensitive, as we see happening with DNA evidence, and the information that can be gleaned increases in size, as we see happening with digital evidence, the role of the expert is only going to become increasingly more difficult. To read and analyse large amounts of digital or other scientific evidences, understand and communicate the findings to an audience who may have very little background in the area is challenging, and to do that in full view of the press adds further stress. How the role of the expert responds to these challenges will be interesting to watch.

Notes

1. Criminal Procedure Rules 2005, Part 19.
2. Ibid.
3. COPFS Guidance Booklet for Expert Witnesses [http://www.copfs.gov.uk/images/Documents/Prosecution_Policy_Guidance/Guidelines_and_Policy/Guidance%20booklet%20for%20expert%20witnesses.PDF] accessed 26/11/2018, Disclosure – Experts' Evidence, Case Management and Unused Material, May 2010: Guidance Booklet for Experts [https://www.cps.gov.uk/legal-guidance/disclosure-experts-evidence-case-management-and-unused-material-may-2010-guidance] accessed 26/11/2018.
4. Criminal Procedure Rules 2005, Part 19.
5. *Cutler v Dixon* (1585) 4 6 Rep 14b.
6. *Jones v Kaney* [2011] UKSC 13.
7. [2011] UKSC 13.

Ethics and the Role of the Expert Witness

1

TONY WARD

Contents

The ethical obligations of a witness called upon to give expert opinion evidence are more complex than just telling 'the truth, the whole truth and nothing but the truth'. Indeed, one of the traditional legal objections to opinion evidence – evidence about the inferences a witness draws from facts – is that dishonest opinion evidence would escape the law of perjury.[1] The main theme of this chapter is that as well as being truthful, experts have an obligation to express *justified* opinions and to make the facts, assumptions and methods on which those opinions are based as *transparent* as possible. These obligations are inherent in the role that the expert witness voluntarily accepts (it is rare for an expert to testify under compulsion). They also reflect the obligation in the Code of Conduct for Forensic Practitioners (Forensic Science Regulator 2017) to 'act with honesty, integrity, objectivity and impartiality'.

It is mainly the judges who authoritatively define what is expected of an expert witness, and nowadays in England and Wales – though not to the same extent in Scotland – these expectations are largely codified in the Criminal Procedure Rules (Crim PR) as well as the guidance contained in some leading judgements. In accepting the role of an expert witness, a practitioner incurs a *prima facie* obligation to meet those legally defined obligations, and thus law is often an important guide to ethics (Willis 2009). On the other hand, legal guidance should be interpreted as far as possible so that it makes good ethical sense.

1.1 Fidelity and Trust

The moral philosopher W. D. Ross brought telling the truth and keeping explicit or implicit promises together as a category of *prima facie* 'duties of fidelity' (Ross 2002: 21). The maker of an ostensibly factual communication gives an implicit assurance that it is true (Moran 2006), and the duty to honour this assurance by telling the truth is an aspect of the duty to keep promises. Duties of fidelity in Ross's sense make up most of the ethical obligations of an expert witness.

An expert witness – and particularly a forensic scientist – is relied upon by the court to examine certain evidence and draw inferences from it that the court could not draw for itself. The epistemic dependence of the court on the expert creates special responsibilities. Joseph Sanders argues that the central duty of the expert is to hold and express justified beliefs:

> When we say that we believe something to be true, we are warranting our commitment to the truth of a proposition (the belief condition) and that we are entitled to this belief (the justification condition). … It is irresponsible to assert knowledge without adequate justification. Behavior that is irresponsible in this way is unethical when it occurs within settings where individuals hold themselves (and their representatives) out as having knowledge upon which others rely. It is unethical for expert witnesses to hold or express unjustified beliefs.
>
> **(Sanders 2007: 1541–2)**

Sanders's view raises a thorny philosophical issue about whether people have the sort of voluntary control over their beliefs that is necessary for moral responsibility (Steup 2001), and it seems to erase the distinction between acting unethically and making an honest mistake. Rather than being ethically obliged to *hold* only justified beliefs, experts have a duty to follow practices of inquiry that ensure, as far as is reasonably practicable, that they *form* only justified beliefs. Thus, they should examine all – and only – the available evidence relevant to their task, analyse it conscientiously and impartially, and do their best to avoid perceptual, logical or mathematical errors. In Steven Lubet's view, the 'single most important obligation of an expert witness is to approach each question with independence and objectivity' (Lubet 1999: 467).

Because of the epistemic dependence of courts, and laypeople in general, on experts, relations between them 'rest on an ineluctable element of *trust*' (Hardwig 1994: 89). Experts must not abuse the trust placed in them and must not 'undermine the attempts of laypersons to be rational' (Ibid: 90). In short, experts must be trustworthy. But in the case of expert witnesses, that trustworthiness must be of a particular kind.

Paul Faulkner (2011) has distinguished between two kinds of trust which he terms 'predictive' and 'affective'. Predictive trust involves relying on someone to do what we have some inductive reason for thinking they are likely to do. For example, I may trust someone to give me good advice if they have often given me good advice about similar matters in the past. Affective trust, on the other hand, goes beyond what one has inductive reasons to expect, and is bestowed because it is appropriate to relationships characterised by norms of trust. For example, I tend to believe what my students tell me about their reasons for missing classes because it would undermine the relationship between us if I constantly doubted their word (and because the truth or otherwise of their excuses is relatively unimportant). I run a risk of being deceived, but a risk that I judge to be acceptable. Ordinary social relationships are characterised by reciprocal expectations that one party will tell the truth and the other will believe them, unless there is some particular reason to doubt them. But relations between witnesses and fact-finders are not like that.

This is especially true in the case of prosecution witnesses testifying in a criminal trial. The jury's duty is to acquit the defendant unless the evidence makes them sure of guilt (subject to certain exceptions where the burden of proof is placed on the defence). Jurors do not have the sort of relationship with experts in which the expert has an expectation of being believed simply on the strength of her implicit assurance that what she says is correct. Nor are they entitled to take the risks inherent in affective trust when those risks will be borne by the defendant rather than themselves. The jury, therefore, should not believe the expert unless they have good positive reasons to believe that what the expert says is true, and experts should not try to persuade juries to have greater confidence in their opinions than is warranted by the evidence of the experts' reliability. The relation between a witness and the jury lacks the reciprocity of trust to be found in ordinary social relationships: the witness has a strong obligation to tell the truth, without any legitimate expectation that the jury will take her word for it. This is true not just of experts but of all witnesses, and is one reason why giving evidence is often a distressing experience for ordinary witnesses, and why the court is sometimes experienced by experts as a site of 'institutionalized pure mistrust' (Wynne 1989: 33).

Experts who are skilled witnesses may be able to overcome this mistrust through their ability to develop a rapport with the jury. But trial outcomes should not be determined by which expert has the greater 'charisma' or the better 'chemistry' with the jury (House of Commons 2005: paras. 140–2). The proverbially effective courtroom performances of the pathologist Sir Bernard Spilsbury, coupled with his often unjustifiably dogmatic opinions, now appear highly suspect from an ethical point of view (Rose 2007).

The responsibility of experts is not to persuade juries to trust them, but rather to provide the juries with the evidence on which to base an independent judgement of how far to trust them. This is made explicit in the famous Scottish case (often cited in the English courts) of *Davie v Edinburgh Corporation* 1952 SLT 54:

> Their duty is to furnish the Judge or jury with the necessary scientific criteria for testing the accuracy of their conclusions, so as to enable the Judge or jury to form their own independent judgment by the application of these criteria to the facts proved in evidence. ... The bare *ipse dixit* of a scientist, however eminent, upon the issue in controversy, will normally carry little weight, for it cannot be tested by cross-examination nor independently appraised, and the parties have invoked the decision of a judicial tribunal and not an oracular pronouncement by an expert.
>
> **(p. 57)**

The same principle is encapsulated in a more recent Scottish judgement: the evidence 'must follow a developed methodology which is explicable and open to possible challenge, and it must produce a result which is capable of being assessed and given more or less weight in light of all the evidence before the finder of fact'.[2] An 'ethical habit' of 'transparency' (Candilis et al. 2007: 17) should lead experts to explain their reasoning in such a way as to facilitate these processes of challenge and assessment.

1.2 Ethics and the Criminal Procedure Rules

The ethical duty of transparency is made explicit in the (English) Criminal Procedure Rules 2015 (Crim PR), r. 19.4, which stipulates the contents of an expert's report. Among other requirements, the report must:

(f) where there is a range of opinion on the matters dealt with in the report—
  (i) summarise the range of opinion, and
  (ii) give reasons for the expert's own opinion;
(g) if the expert is not able to give an opinion without qualification, state the qualification.

Although no equivalent rules exist in Scotland, the courts appear to have similar expectations. In *Wilson v HMA* (2009) HCJAC 58 the Appeal Court endorsed the guidance set out in *The Ikarian Reefer* (1993) 2 Lloyd's Rep 68, the source of many of the principles now contained in the Crim PR. The forensic anthropologists who testified in *HMA v Hainey* (2013) HCJAC 47 were criticised for 'refrain[ing] from making any reference to apparently respectable scientific writing in the field which had the effect of seriously qualifying their views' (para. 50), as they would have been required to do in England by both Crim PR r. 19.4(f) and (g). In any case, transparency about such matters is a clear ethical obligation. An expert speaks with the authority of a particular profession or branch of knowledge and where no contrary indication is given may reasonably be assumed to speak for that profession or branch of knowledge as a whole. It is misleading and therefore unethical to give that impression where the community of experts is in fact divided (Hardwig 1994: 92).

An additional requirement of Crim PR 19.4, first introduced in 2014, is that a report must

> (h) include such information as the court may need to decide whether the expert's opinion is sufficiently reliable to be admissible as evidence.

This requirement is designed to achieve partial implementation of the Law Commission's (2011) report on expert evidence, in conjunction with the Practice Direction which guides judges as to the matters to be taken into account in assessing reliability. The test of 'sufficient reliability' is a common law one, not the new statutory test proposed by the Law Commission (2011). In essence, it requires that the expert's evidence is based on a body of knowledge that is sufficiently reliable to be of assistance to the jury, and that rationally supports the conclusions drawn from it. The precise interpretation of the legal test of admissibility is beyond the scope of this chapter (see Ward 2015), but it largely coincides (at least it should) with the expert's ethical duty to follow methods of inquiry that will lead to justified beliefs.

As an ethical as well as a legal matter, experts should use only 'methods of demonstrable validity', as the Forensic Science Regulator's (FSR) (2017) Code of Conduct puts it, and should draw only conclusions that are rationally supported by those methods. 'Demonstrable validity', however, is a question of degree. For example, facial identification by video superimposition could be considered self-evidently valid in the sense that the similarities or differences between faces can be clearly seen on the screen; what has not been clearly demonstrated is *how* valid or accurate such similarities are as a means of identification (Edmond et al. 2009). It is not necessarily unethical, nor will it necessarily result in evidence being inadmissible, to express opinions based on techniques of this sort, provided that the expert clearly acknowledges the limitations of the research and the possibilities of error.[3]

Where the reliability of a technique has been questioned in the published literature, this should (as r. 19.4(f) requires in England and Wales) be drawn to the attention of the court (see *HMA v Hainey* above). A report should set out 'any material facts or matters which detract from the expert's opinions and any points which should fairly be made against any opinions expressed'.[4] This is essential both because the adversary system is not so consistently effective that it can be relied upon to expose any flaws in expert evidence, and because an expert's primary duty is to the court rather than to one of the parties.

As is spelt out in r. 19.2, an expert's duty is to help the court to achieve the overriding objective of dealing with cases justly (r. 1.1), and that duty overrides any duty to the party instructing the expert. To underline the point, r. 19.4(j) requires the expert's report to 'contain a statement that the expert understands an expert's duty to the court, and has complied and will continue to comply with that duty'. To their credit, the Association of Chief Police Officers (ACPO) and the Crown Prosecution Service (CPS) in their guidance to expert witnesses (2010) strongly emphasise the expert's overriding duty to the court (see also CPS, n.d.). Similar guidance is given by the Crown Office and Prosecutor Fiscal Service (n.d.: 2) in Scotland.

1.3 Keeping within One's Expertise

The FSR Code of Conduct for Forensic Practitioners enjoins scientists to 'provide expert advice and evidence only within the limits of your professional competence'. The ethical importance of this obligation when giving evidence follows from the principle that the role of the expert is to put the fact-finder in a position to make an accurate and independent judgement of the weight of the evidence. Experts who stray beyond their area of competence increase their risk of making errors and also convey to the jury a misleading impression of the weight of their opinions. Experts may trespass on the expertise of other professions or – a matter of equal if not greater concern to the courts – they may stray into areas that the law does not consider to be matters of expert opinion at all.

The boundaries of any particular field of expertise are not always clearly defined. A recurring feature of the history of the professions is that two or more specialisms will claim expertise in a particular area, and one or more claimants will seek to define such expertise as its sole prerogative (Abbott 1988). In a case such as *HMA v Hainey* it is not obvious (from a lay perspective) that whether features of human bones are indicative of malnutrition is solely a medical matter and not also within the domain of physical anthropology. Faced with such uncertainty, it may seem reasonable for experts to leave it to lawyers and judges to determine the limits within which their evidence is legally relevant. The Crim PR, however, could hardly be more emphatic in stating that it is the expert's duty to 'help the court … by giving opinion … which is within the expert's area or areas of expertise', to define that area of expertise both in their report and in oral evidence, and 'to draw the court's attention to any question to which the answer would be outside the expert's area or areas of expertise' (r. 19.2(1) and (3)(b)).

The relation between law and professional ethics in this respect was discussed by the Court of Appeal in reviewing the General Medical Council's (GMC) finding that Professor Sir Roy Meadow had committed serious professional misconduct by his evidence in the Sally Clarke murder trial. Auld LJ noted that there is 'much overlap' between an expert's duty to the court and that to uphold the ethical standards of his profession, 'but, in the hurly-burly of the trial process, especially seen through the eyes of the expert witness they may not, in practice, always complement each other'.[5] The fact that Meadow had been led astray by counsel's questions and the ineffective performance of defence counsel and the trial judge was a mitigating factor sufficient, in the view of Auld and Thorpe LJJ (but not Clarke MR) to reduce his offence from serious professional misconduct to mere professional misconduct, but it did not absolve him from responsibility. Indeed, the fact that even senior counsel and judges sometimes do such a poor job of patrolling the boundaries of expertise makes it all the more important for experts to police themselves, especially in routine cases where standards of advocacy and judging may be even lower.

1.4 Integrity, Objectivity and Impartiality

According to the FSR Code of Practice, forensic practitioners should act 'with honesty, integrity, objectivity and impartiality'. Honesty has already been discussed, but what do the other three virtues require?

Integrity is perhaps the hardest of the professional virtues to define. According to Beauchamp and Childress (2013: 40) it involves both 'a coherent integration of aspects of the self – emotions, aspirations, knowledge and the like – so that each complements and does not frustrate the other' and 'the character trait of being faithful to moral values and standing up in their defense when necessary'. In the context of scientific activity, it involves above all an unswerving commitment to truth: trying 'to get it right at all costs, sparing no effort' (Holton 2005: 91).

In the first of Beauchamp and Childress's two senses, an expert witness forsakes integrity if, when his or her 'reputation or *amour propre* is at stake', these aspirations and emotions frustrate the pursuit of truth.[6] In the second sense, integrity involves both a willingness to stick to one's guns and the humility to acknowledge that one may be mistaken and others may have greater expertise. Experts must not allow pressure from the party instructing them to divert them from their duty to the court, but they should also beware of allowing pressures to reach agreement to lead them to make greater concessions than the interests of justice require. This is a danger that could arise when experts are required by the judge to meet and prepare a statement on the areas on which they agree and disagree. In the civil case of *Jones v Kaney* (2011) UKSC 13, the defendant had signed a joint statement by the experts in an action for personal injury, which she later admitted did not reflect her true opinion and which undermined her client's claim for damages. The Supreme Court decided that expert witnesses did not enjoy immunity from suit for breach of their duty to the party instructing them – and this might also apply to a defence expert in a criminal case (Ibid., paras. 60, 125).

A particularly delicate situation arises where an expert is confronted with an opposing opinion from another expert who has more specialised knowledge on the relevant aspect of the case. In *A Local Authority v S* (2009) EWHC 2115 (Fam), a civil case on 'shaken baby syndrome', King J said that 'each expert must defer to the expertise of others more qualified to comment on certain areas ... not grudgingly or reluctantly, but in ready acknowledgement of the greater expertise and knowledge that the other specialists may have' (para. 254). An expert, however, can be under no greater obligation than a jury to defer blindly to the opinions of someone with greater expertise. Professional etiquette, or fear of displeasing the judge, should not deter an expert from insisting, with due respect to a more knowledgeable colleague, that she finds the latter's views unconvincing.

Objectivity and impartiality are closely related values: indeed, impartiality can be considered one aspect of objectivity (Kramer 2007: 2, 46–7), which may be why the European Network of Forensic Science Institutes (ENFSI 2005) Code of Conduct limits its list of virtues to 'honesty, objectivity and integrity', omitting impartiality as a separate value. Ideally, impartiality requires that the expert has nothing at stake in the proceedings. In reality, this ideal state of affairs can rarely if ever exist in an adversarial trial. Even if experts resist every temptation to identify with the prosecution or defence 'team', they may come sincerely to believe in the defendant's guilt or innocence, and thus to have a stake in securing what they regard as a just result. Even if they remain neutral on that matter, they still have a stake in convincing the jury of the truth of their own conclusions, which gives them an incentive to ignore or downplay points that count against those conclusions. Their own reputation as a competent expert and effective witness will often be at stake, and so in many cases will be the competitive position of their employer. A more realistic view of impartiality, then, is that it requires that what one has at stake should not colour one's evidence. Some ethicists and practitioners doubt whether even that ideal is fully attainable (Candilis et al. 2007). The ethics code for U.S. forensic psychiatrists requires them only to 'strive for objectivity' (AAPL 2005: section IV).

The FSR Code of Practice goes into some detail about the conflicts of interest and other 'threats to impartiality' that a forensic practitioner may face (Forensic Science Regulator 2017: para. 7.1.2). Conflicts of interest include being (or perceiving oneself to be) coerced, being asked to disregard critical findings that support or undermine the prosecution or defence, or having a close personal or financial relationship with someone likely to be affected by the outcome of a case, or with another expert witness in the case. The crucial legal/ethical principle about such conflicts of interest is that they must be brought to the court's attention at the first opportunity.[7]

Other 'threats to impartiality' mentioned in the code include being the sole reviewer of one's own critical findings. The same might also be said of reviewing a colleague's findings in full knowledge of the colleague's opinion (Risinger et al. 2002). The Code of Practice requires only that 'where the forensic unit has deemed', for example as a result of a validation study, that an independent check is required, the supplier should define the level of independence required and keep records to demonstrate it (para. 15.3.3). The Forensic Science Regulator (2015) goes significantly further: 'Independent checking that minimizes the risk of cognitive bias would entail assessment without knowing the outcome of the initial analysis, or even where practicable the identity of the original examiner in order to avoid confirmation bias' (para. 4.4.8).

The Code of Practice echoes the Court of Appeal decision in *R v Momodou* (2005) EWCA Crim 177 in condemning anything that could be construed as witness coaching, as distinct from familiarisation, as a threat to impartiality. As explained in *Momodou*, this

> principle does not prohibit training of expert and similar witnesses in, for example, the technique of giving comprehensive evidence of a specialist kind to a jury, both during evidence-in-chief and in cross-examination, and, another example, developing the ability to resist the inevitable pressure of going further in evidence than matters covered by the witnesses' specific expertise. The critical feature of training of this kind is that it should not be arranged in the context of nor related to any forthcoming trial, and it can therefore have no impact whatever on it.
>
> **(para. 62)**

The Code of Practice also refers to the dangers of 'being over-familiar with or trusting another person instead of relying on objective evidence'. Presumably the sort of people the Code has in view are police officers, lawyers, the defendant or the complainant. But this barely scratches the surface of the much bigger ethical problem which the Regulator addresses in the *Draft Guidance*: the question of how far the forensic scientist should work as part of an investigative team. Focusing on the scientist's role in the *investigation* of major crime, Barclay (2009: 339) makes a strong case for a 'completely integrated approach' to major criminal investigations, 'with detectives, crime analysts, forensic scientists, pathologists and behavioural experts all part of the same team'. If, however, we focus on the scientist's role as *witness*, the integrated approach appears ethically problematic:

> When the forensic scientist is exposed to, relies on, or is influenced by any information outside of her own domain, she is abusing her warrant, even though she may honestly believe that such information makes her conclusion more reliable, and even, or especially, if she is right about this. Her role is not to give a conclusion based even partly on information outside her domain, which the jury can presumptively evaluate at least as well as she, but only to give the jury the reliable product of her discipline that is beyond what they could deduce on their own.
>
> **(Risinger et al. 2002: 28)**

Willis (2009) argues that the value of an integrative approach is not that it generates more reliable answers, but rather that it can ensure that scientists ask the right questions. It appears that the best solution to the ethical quandary may be to separate the task of asking the questions from that of providing the answers, and this is just what is envisaged in Regulator's *Guidance*(2015). The person responsible for deciding the analytical strategy should have all the information regarding the case, while the person who does the actual analysis should have no more information than is relevant to that task (para. 4.4.23). Background information can then be re-introduced for the purpose of interpreting the results in the light of relevant hypotheses. It is acknowledged, however, that this approach will not always be practicable (para. 5.1.4). Where it is not, the best solution might be to ensure blind checking of the practitioner's work by someone without contextual information.

If impartiality is one aspect of objectivity, the other is the sense in which evidence is 'objective' if it reflects the conclusions that any competent inquirer would arrive at given the data available to the expert and the knowledge shared by experts in the relevant field. By contrast, 'subjective' evidence reflects the expert's personal experience or her preference for one of a range of possibilities in a situation where other experts might reasonably make a different choice. In this sense, objectivity is a property of the evidence, not a virtue of the witness. To give evidence that is coloured by personal experience or a reasonable preference is not, in itself, an ethical failing (Jackson et al. 2014: 88). The ethical failing is to present evidence as being objective when it is not. To avoid this requires what might be termed 'second-order objectivity': the ability to recognise the objective limits of objectivity in one's field.

The concern that the limits of expert objectivity should be clearly conveyed to the jury is a theme of three of the most important recent judgements on forensic science evidence: *R v Atkins* (2009) EWCA Crim 1876; *R v Reed* (2009) EWCA Crim 2698; and *R v T (Footwear Mark Evidence)*

(2010) EWCA Crim 2439. In all these judgements the Court of Appeal distinguishes between calculations of probability that are 'objective' in the sense of being derived from a dataset that any expert would be expected to use, and estimates that are 'subjective' in the sense of being based on the expert's own experience or (as in *T*) on a choice between two or more datasets which will yield different results. All the judgements stress that when an objective basis for an estimate of probability is lacking, the expert must make this clear to the jury. In order to ensure that this is done, the evidence must be set out in the expert's report 'in the terms in which it is to be given', so that the judge can rule in advance of the trial whether evidence given in those terms will be admissible.[8] In this respect, the judgements simply reinforce the ethical duty of the expert to avoid misleading the jury.

R v T, however, goes further in suggesting that an expert should say merely that a shoe 'could have made' a mark (para. 73). To say that a shoe 'could have made' a mark, without any indication of how many other shoes could have made the same mark, is so uninformative and potentially misleading that it is arguably unethical (Jackson et al. 2014: 39). What the court apparently had in mind was the American terminology in which 'could have made' indicates 'a significant association of multiple class characteristics' (para. 66). As that is obviously not what 'could have made' means in plain English, an expert using the phrase in this artificial sense would be telling less than 'the whole truth' if she failed to define it and explain what she meant by 'significant association' and 'class characteristics'. If the aim is to convey the limits of objective knowledge, it might be better for the expert to say that only a small minority of shoes would make similar marks, but she can offer only a subjective estimate of how small that minority is. The important point to take from this passage in *R v T* is that phrases like 'moderate scientific support' should be avoided where they disguise the element of subjectivity involved in an expert judgement.

It is unfortunate that the *R v T* case has called into question some aspects of the Case Assessment and Interpretation (CAI) approach which, if implemented appropriately, would satisfy several important ethical requirements (Jackson et al. 2014). It should encourage experts to take account impartially of both prosecution and defence hypotheses, to distinguish clearly between the results of their analyses and assumptions made in interpreting them, and to make clear when they are basing probability calculations on specific data and when they are relying on rough estimates. At the same time, it is important to appreciate why this approach may give rise to judicial anxiety. A fundamental common law principle is that it is for juries to determine the weight of expert evidence, not for the experts themselves. What I suspect – though this is not clearly expressed in the *R v T* judgement – raises judicial hackles about CAI is that the experts appear to be offering an objective-looking measure of the weight of their own evidence. If this is cloaked in the 'verisimilitude of mathematical probability'[9] the jury may feel – or so the judges fear – that they are not in a position to question it. It is therefore vital that the results of CAI are presented in a way that reveals whatever uncertainties exist in the underlying science as clearly as possible for a lay audience and avoids any suspicion of blinding the jury with statistics.

1.5 Transparency and the Adversarial Process

As we have seen, the key ethical tension in the role of an expert witness is that she is a participant in an adversarial process but her first duty is not to either party but to the court, and this may require her to assist in undermining her own evidence. This is less of paradox than it might appear at first sight. The chief virtue of the adversarial system is that it promotes sceptical examination of the evidence, including expert evidence. The expert's obligation, in keeping with both scientific and legal values, is to facilitate this goal by presenting her evidence in a transparent fashion that opens it up to sceptical scrutiny. This is what the reporting protocol used by the expert in *R v T*, by failing to explain the calculations by which the judgement of 'moderate scientific support' was reached, conspicuously failed to do (Redmayne et al. 2011: 349).

There are two other areas where this duty of transparency is important. One is the prosecution expert's role in the pre-trial disclosure process (ACPO and CPS 2010; Crown Office and Prosecutor Fiscal Service, n.d.). The other is that information that is necessary to the critical scrutiny of expert evidence must be disclosed notwithstanding issues of commercial confidentiality (CPS, n.d.). As the lord chief justice recently stated:

> Where a development in forensic science is used in court, information that goes to the reliability of the technical or scientific method used must be put into the public domain and made available to all. That is because in relation to the use of such science in criminal justice, commercial considerations of a kind which might ordinarily be applicable must take second place to the provision of all material which is relevant to establishing innocence or proving guilt.
>
> **(Thomas 2014: para. 28)**

In conclusion, while the obligation to give truthful, justified and transparent testimony with integrity and objectivity may appear simple, it can be onerous, especially when experts' duty to the court is in tension with their roles as commercial service providers or as members of an investigative, prosecution or defence team.

Notes

1. *Adams v Cannon* [1621] Dyer 117.
2. *Young v HMA* [2013] HCJAC 145, para. 54.
3. See *R v Atkins* [2009] EWCA Crim 1876.
4. *R v B* [2006] EWCA Crim 417, para. 177; see also *R v Ward* [1996] 93 Cr App R 1, p. 56.
5. *Meadow v GMC* [2006] EWCA Civ 1390, para. 204.
6. *Re U (a Child)* [2004] EWCA Civ 567, para. 23.
7. *Toth v Jarman* [2006] EWCA Civ 1028 paras. 112–3.
8. *R v Reed*, para. 121.
9. *R v T*, para. 86.

References

AAPL (American Academy of Psychiatry and Law). 2005. *Ethics Guidelines for the Practice of Forensic Psychiatry.* http://www.aapl.org/ethics.htm (accessed 11 Feb. 2012).

Abbott, A. 1988. *The System of Professions.* Chicago: University of Chicago Press.

ACPO (Association of Chief Police Officers) and CPS (Crown Prosecution Service). 2010. *Disclosure: Experts' Evidence and Unused Material. Guidance Booklet for Experts.* https://www.cps.gov.uk/legal-guidance/disclosure-experts-evidence-case-management-and-unused-material-may-2010-guidance (accessed 25th January 2019).

Barclay, D. 2009. Using forensic science in major crime inquiries. In *Handbook of Forensic Science* (pp. 359–380), ed. J. Fraser and R. Williams. Cullompton, Devon: Willan.

Beauchamp, T. L. and J. F. Childress. 2013. *Principles of Biomedical Ethics* (7th ed.). Oxford: Oxford University Press.

Candilis, P. J., R. L. Weinstock and R. Martinez. 2007. *Forensic Ethics and the Expert Witness.* New York: Springer.

CPS (Crown Prosecution Service). n.d. *Core Foundation Principles for Forensic Science Providers.* https://www.cps.gov.uk/legal-guidance/core-foundation-principles-forensic-science-providers (accessed 25th January 2019).

Crown Office and Prosecutor Fiscal Service. n.d. *Guidance Booklet for Expert Witnesses: The Role of the Expert Witness and Disclosure.* Available from www.copfs.gov.uk (accessed 30 Dec. 2014).

Edmond, G., K. Biber, R. Kemp and G. Porter. 2009. Law's looking glass: expert identification evidence derived from photographic and video images. *Current Issues in Criminal Justice* 20: 337–77.

ENFSI (European Network of Forensic Science Institutes). 2005. *Code of Conduct.* http://enfsi.eu/wp-content/uploads/2016/09/code_of_conduct.pdf (accessed 25th January 2019).

Faulkner, P. 2011. *Knowledge on Trust.* Oxford: Oxford University Press.

Forensic Science Regulator. 2015. *Guidance: Cognitive Bias Effects Relevant to Forensic Science Examinations.* https://www.gov.uk/government/publications/cognitive-bias-effects-relevant-to-forensic-science-examinations (accessed 19 Sept. 2016).

Forensic Science Regulator. 2017. *Codes of Practice and Conduct for Forensic Service Providers and Practitioners in the Criminal Justice System* (Issue 4). https://www.gov.uk/government/publications/forensic-science-providers-codes-of-practice-and-conduct-2017 (accessed 19 Feb 2019).

Hardwig, J. 1994. Toward an ethics of expertise. In *Professional Ethics and Social Responsibility* (pp. 83–101), ed. D. E. Wueste. Lanham, MD: Rowman & Littlefield.

Holton, G. 2005. Candor and integrity in science. In *Scientific Virtues and Civic Values* (pp 277–294) ed. N. Koertge. Oxford: Oxford University Press.

House of Commons, Science and Technology Committee. 2005. *Forensic Science on Trial: 7th Report of the Session 2004–5* (HC 96-i). London: The Stationery Office.

Jackson, G., C. Aitken and P. Roberts. 2014. *Practitioner Guide No. 4: Case Assessment and Interpretation of Expert Evidence*. London: Royal Statistical Society.

Kramer, M. 2007. *Objectivity and the Rule of Law*. Cambridge: Cambridge University Press.

Law Commission. 2011. *Expert Evidence in Criminal Proceedings* (Law Com No. 325). https://www.lawcom.gov.uk/project/expert-evidence-in-criminal-proceedings/(accessed 25th January 2019).

Lubet, S. 1999. Expert witnesses: ethics and professionalism. *Georgetown Journal of Legal Ethics* 12: 465–88.

Moran, R. 2006. Getting told and being believed. In *The Epistemology of Testimony* (pp. 272–306), ed. J. Lackey and E. Sosa. Oxford: Oxford University Press.

Redmayne, M., P., Roberts, C. Aitken and G. Jackson. 2011. Forensic science evidence in question. *Criminal Law Review* (5): 347–56.

Risinger, D. M., M. J. Saks, R. C. Thompson and R. Rosenthal. 2002. The *Daubert/Kumho* implications of observer effects in forensic science: hidden problems of expectation and suggestion. *Southern California Law Review* 90: 1–56.

Rose, A. 2007. *Lethal Witness: Sir Bernard Spilsbury, Honorary Pathologist*. Kent, OH: Kent State University Press.

Ross, W. D. 2002. *The Right and the Good*. Oxford: Oxford University Press (originally published 1930).

Sanders, J. 2007. Expert witness ethics. *Fordham Law Review* 76: 1535–84.

Steup, M. (ed.). 2001. *Knowledge, Truth and Duty*. Oxford: Oxford University Press.

Lord Thomas of Cwmgiedd. 2014. *The Future of Forensic Science in Criminal Trials*. http://www.judiciary.gov.uk/wp-content/uploads/2014/10/kalisher-lecture-expert-evidence-oct-14.pdf (accessed 31 Dec. 2014).

Ward, T. 2015. 'A new and more rigorous approach' to expert evidence in England and Wales? *International Journal of Evidence & Proof* 19(4): 228–45.

Willis, S. 2009. Forensic science, ethics and criminal justice. In *Handbook of Forensic Science* (pp. 523–546), ed. J. Fraser and R. Williams. Cullompton, Devon: Willan.

Wynne, B. 1989. Establishing the rules of laws: constructing expert authority. In *Expert Evidence: Interpreting Science in the Law*, ed. R. Smith and B. Wynne. London: Routledge.

The Impact of Case Law and Inquiries on the Role of the Expert Witness

2

TOM WELSH

Contents

2.1 The Context

This chapter deals with the case law as it has developed, principally in Scotland. Usually (but not always), an expert witness is a stranger to the material facts, the parties and the key issues in the case. The typical expert is a person of medical, scientific, technological, academic or practical skill, knowledge, experience and/or standing, who is consulted by parties, some time, possibly years, after the event, issue or occurrence in dispute has transpired. That consultation will be in the course of preparation for a disputed legal proof, whether that is in a civil claim or a criminal trial. An expert can be but is typically not 'a witness to fact'. Usually, the facts are established independently of the expert's opinion. He or she expresses that opinion in the case, not in the abstract but in relation to the case as pled or presented and on the basis that certain specific facts asserted by parties in anticipation of proof are, in fact, established at proof and accepted so by the trier of fact to the requisite legal standard. Of course, experts' opinions are not determinative and as is well understood, they may be discarded altogether by the trier of fact, or one expert preferred over another. Thus, arguably the most significant Scottish case in relation to expert evidence, *Davie v Magistrates of Edinburgh*,[1] decided in the mid-twentieth century, in so far as it articulates the crucial distinction between the role of the expert and the role of the judge and/or jury, continues to play an important part in the definition and demarcation of the forensic landscape within the courtroom today. In that case, Lord President Cooper articulated a rule that lawyers readily comprehend which clearly defines and restricts the role of the expert within the legal process. The expert may triumph in the laboratory and be lauded within the scientific community but yet still fail within the courtroom and be rejected by a judge or jury. The rule, put shortly, is that an expert's opinion can only *inform* the final decision, but importantly, it can never *form* that decision. The ultimate issue is always for the court to decide.[2] The expert's opinion cannot supplant the judicial function:[3]

> Expert witnesses, however skilled or eminent can give no more than evidence. They cannot usurp the functions of the jury or the Judge sitting as a jury … their duty is to furnish the Judge or jury with the necessary specific scientific criteria for testing the accuracy of their conclusions so as to enable the Judge or jury to form their own independent judgement by the application of these criteria to the facts proved in evidence. The scientific opinion evidence, if intelligible, convincing and tested, becomes a factor (and often an important factor) for consideration along with the whole other evidence in the case, but the decision is for the Judge or jury. In particular the bare *ipse dixit* of a scientist, however, eminent, upon the issue in controversy, will normally carry little weight, for it cannot be tested by cross-examined nor independently appraised and the parties have invoked the decision of a judicial tribunal and not an oracular pronouncement by an expert.

The pre-eminent position that experts enjoy in the natural world as harbingers of truth based upon experiment, discovery and reason is necessarily relegated to a secondary status in the legal world, because they proffer but 'mere' opinion evidence and do not decide the case, which is a judicial function. It is not uncommon to hear a judge direct a civil or criminal jury that Professor X or Dr Y gave certain evidence '… but remember, ladies and gentlemen, that was, *only*, their opinion. They were not present. Their function is only to inform and advise you on the technical or scientific aspects of the present case, if you choose to accept their analysis. However, they did not see what happened. They have not heard all the evidence you have. They do not decide the case'. Thus, the respective functions of the judge and jury and the expert are separate and distinct. It was put this way by Professor Wilkinson in discussing the passage from the lord president cited above:

> The point that Lord President Cooper was concerned to make is sometimes overlooked. The function of the expert is not to present ready-made conclusions but to provide the tribunal of fact with material on which it can reach its own conclusions. The decision on the various issues in the case, including the issues of fact in the resolution of which the expert may assist,

> is for the judge or jury. The expert must not usurp their function. On the basis of that perception, it has been said "a question is inadmissible if its purpose is to elicit an opinion on the actual issue before the court". The principle is reasonably clear and intelligible. Judges and juries have their functions and experts have theirs. The expert who crosses the line dividing these functions ceases to assist, and usurps. … While court or jury are to be furnished with criteria on which to make their independent judgment it is clear that that judgment is to be applied to conclusions which experts have themselves reached. The court will inevitably want to know how the expert has applied the criteria to the facts in order to reach his conclusion. There is, therefore, much ground which both the expert and court or jury must traverse together. The problem of whether a particular question or piece of evidence transgresses unacceptably on the province of judge or jury does not admit of an easy answer.
>
> **(Wilkinson, *The Scottish Law of Evidence*, pp 65–66)**

Both the scientist and the courts strive to ascertain the truth; however, they are working in very different but occasionally aligned paradigms, using very similar language for radically different concepts. This can cause confusion. What passes for proof and consistency in the court is not the same as in the laboratory. These two worlds normally live in total harmony but have the capacity to collide in the courtroom with catastrophic consequences for justice. An American Supreme Court justice who had a great passion for science understood the distinction and put it rather well in *Daubert v Merrell Dow Pharmaceuticals Inc*[4] when he explained the need for courts to exclude some important aspects of scientific inquiry for reasons of legal pragmatism:

> It is true that open debate is an essential part of both legal and scientific analyses. Yet there are important differences between the quest for truth in the courtroom and the quest for truth in the laboratory. Scientific conclusions are subject to perpetual revision. Law, on the other hand, must resolve disputes finally and quickly. The scientific project is advanced by broad and wide ranging consideration of a multitude of hypotheses, for those that are incorrect will eventually be shown to be so, and that in itself is an advance. Conjectures that are probably wrong are of little use, however, in the project of reaching a quick, final, and binding legal judgment – often of great consequence – about a particular set of events in the past. We recognize that in practice, a gatekeeping role for the judge, no matter how flexible, inevitably on occasion will prevent the jury from learning of authentic insights and innovations. That, nevertheless, is the balance that is struck by Rules of Evidence designed not for the exhaustive search for cosmic understanding but for the particularized resolution of legal disputes.
>
> **(Justice Harry Blackmun)**

2.2 The Parameters and Constraints of Expert Evidence

The general rule of evidence is that witnesses speak to fact, not hearsay or opinion, after being sworn on oath to tell the truth. Witnesses to fact tell the court what they saw or heard from their direct knowledge. Hearsay is generally excluded. Experts, however, enjoy a privilege in giving evidence. They may express an opinion about matters germane to the inquiry which they have been appraised of which is relevant and material to the inquiry. This privilege is not unlimited; on the contrary, it is closely circumscribed by rules. The opinion expressed must be necessary for the proper determination of the dispute; thus, it must relate to an area of human affairs which the jury could not reasonably be expected to understand, for example, any of the natural or medical sciences. In answering questions, the witness will be expected to show factual and scientific candour and restraint and restrict himself or herself to their own appropriate and relevant area of expertise. To be admitted, the opinion evidence must be necessaryand relevant material for determination of the cause and expressed within the confines of a professional discipline.[5] The witness must be able to demonstrate 'expertise' in the form of skill, knowledge or qualifications. Lord Reed put it thus:

> In general, of course, opinion evidence is not admissible in our criminal courts; witnesses may only under normal circumstances give evidence about matters within their direct knowledge. The evidence of an expert witness is an exception to this rule. It is not possible to provide an absolute direction as to what constitutes legitimate subject matter for expert opinion. However, two general principles will normally give some guidance. Firstly, the subject matter under discussion must be necessary for the proper resolution of the dispute, and be such that a judge or jury without instruction or advice in the particular area of knowledge or experience would be unable to reach a sound conclusion without the help of a witness who had such specialised knowledge or experience. Secondly, the subject matter in question must be part of a recognised body of science or experience which is suitably acknowledged as being useful and reliable, and properly capable of reaching and justifying the opinions offered, and the witness must demonstrate a sufficiently authoritative understanding of the theory and practice of the subject. The nature and scope of expert opinion evidence cannot at any one point in time be exhaustively defined.
>
> (***Wilson v HM Advocate***)[6]

If accredited by the court and admitted as an expert, the witness is not then free to express opinions at large on matters beyond the realm of his or her expertise. On the contrary, further legal restraints apply. An expert is subject to a suite of obligations which further constrain the freedom he or she has to express opinions, and these define the ethical duty which their role entails. It is a cardinal feature of these rules that the expert is not a metaphorical hired gun or 'witness for party', paid to sabotage the opposing case, civil or criminal. Rather, the expert witness must accept that he or she is an expert to the court. This relationship is something similar to that commonly found in the civil law tradition in continental Europe. The expert's role and function there is to assist and guide the court through technical or scientific evidence which the judge could not readily be expected to understand. In civil law systems where an inquisitorial rather than adversarial inquiry is the norm, the expert frequently sits on the bench with the judge advising the court like an assessor, as opposed to giving evidence from the witness box in chief and then under cross-examination. A single expert is frequently, by agreement, appointed by the continental court. The competition between and multiplication of experts which is so common a feature of the common law adversarial system is alien to the continental civil law tradition.

The suite of ethical obligations binding the expert is contained in a shipping case, but it has universal application. In *National Justice Campania Naviera, SA v Prudential Assurance Co. Ltd ('The Ikarion Reefer')*, Cresswell J listed the duties and responsibilities of experts permitted the privilege of expressing an opinion thus:

> 1. Expert evidence presented to the court should be, and should be seen to be, the independent product of the expert uninfluenced as to the form or content by the exigencies of litigation.
> 2. An expert witness should provide independent assistance to the court by way of objective unbiased opinion in relation to matters within his expertise. An expert witness should never assume the role of an advocate.
> 3. An expert witness should state the facts or assumptions on which his opinion is based. He should not omit to consider material facts which could detract from his concluded opinion.
> 4. An expert witness should make it clear when a particular question or issue falls outside his expertise.
> 5. If an expert's opinion is not properly researched because he considers that insufficient data is available, then this must be stated with an indication that the opinion is no more than a provisional one. … In cases where an expert witness who has prepared a report could not assert that the report contained the truth, the whole truth and nothing but the truth without some qualification, that qualification should be stated in the report.

In *Wilson*,[7] the duty was further extended to require of an expert an explanation for the exclusion of any relevant material from his or her professional conclusions.[8] In Scotland, these rules relating to the duties of candour, transparency, restraint and professional independence imposed on experts are not codified as they are in England and Wales, in the Criminal Procedure

Rules and Practice Directions, but they are accepted, at common law, as the appropriate framework within which any expert, in a civil or criminal case, must operate. The court will, in addition, expect parties to take active (case management) steps to reach agreement on non-controversial issues which will *inter alia* include the exchange of reports between experts, for example, in case-managed personal injury cases raised under Chapter 36 of the Ordinary Cause Rules in the sheriff court and their equivalent raised under Chapter 43 of the Rules of the Court of Session. In criminal cases there is a statutory duty of disclosure on the Crown which includes disclosure of expert reports.[9] Thus, today the appearance of an expert and the opinion he or she will give should in the typical case be well heralded and ought to come as no surprise to parties or the trier of fact.

2.3 The Accreditation of the Expert and Admissibility of His Opinion

In Scotland the threshold of admissibility has, until relatively recently, been set quite low as compared to other common law jurisdictions[10] and the judge in this jurisdiction has, traditionally, exercised a weak 'gatekeeper function' to exclude from probation any unsound, invalid or unorthodox opinion. Instead, here, the difficult preliminary question of the quality or soundness of the science or opinion proffered has generally been left to the ultimate trier of fact, whether that be a judge alone or a jury, to assess, as part of the determination of the ultimate issue at stake. The test of admissibility is whether the evidence is necessary, relevant and material. The quality of the opinion expressed has been considered relevant to the ultimate issue rather than the admissibility of the evidence. This weak gatekeeping function, and the *ad hoc* way in which the jurisprudence has developed a low threshold of admissibility, has led to serious problems.

Cases such as *McCreight v HMA* (2009) HCJAC 69, *Liehne v HMA* (2011) HCJAC 51 and *Hainey v HMA* (2013) HCJAC 47 demonstrate the difficulties the courts face in providing adequate instruction to the jury where there are multiple experts offering complex and conflicting opinions and also in addressing fundamental misunderstandings about the scientific basis on which opinions are expressed. However, there are signs emerging of a greater sensitivity on the part of Scottish judges to a more robust gatekeeper function, which may in part be influenced by the improvement of ongoing judicial training among the judges, or a greater awareness among them of the international jurisprudence on this subject.

Judicial scrutiny of the basis upon which expertise is claimed by so-called experts is an important part of the accreditation process. In a case, the Inner House of the Court of Session held that 'an expert' had erroneously been admitted as a witness in a personal injury case, to express opinions about matters well within the cognisance of the first instance court. Lord Brodie put it thus:

> The point is this. A person does not become able to give expert evidence simply by reason of the depth of his knowledge or the width of his experience. The subject matter of that knowledge or experience must be such that it forms part of a generally recognised and specific discipline with a core of organised principle and practice shared by the exponents of that discipline and accordingly amenable to forensic examination and evaluation: *Young v HMA* 2014 SCCR 78 at para 54. As is explained in Lewis, Manual of Evidence in Scotland, at p47, to be relevant a statement of opinion must be "based on the principles of some recognised craft or science in relation to which the witness may be cross-examined." The "craft or science" need not be highly sophisticated. It need not have an extensive associated literature. But it must have identifiable generally accepted principles to which reference can be made. An opinion from someone skilled in such a craft or science may be able to instruct or advise the judge on a particular area of knowledge or experience (to use the language of *Wilson*[11]). Any other sort of opinion is no more than the expression of the personal views of the witness and, as such, of no evidential value.[12]

Of course, what constitutes a generally recognised and specific discipline or a craft or science will in some instances be difficult to determine. Recognised by whom, for how long and in what way? When does a body of knowledge become sufficiently recognised and organised in principle to be considered amenable to forensic examination and evaluation in fact? Which official body validates that recognition and upon what criteria? If it is a court, what skill must the court possess to reach that conclusion? How does this approach deal with 'new science' or 'cutting-edge science' which may, as yet, lack positive peer review or general validation? After all, Galileo's heliocentric theory was only capable of actual verification many years after his death. It was true but rejected because the necessary proof did not exist and could not because of the then general state of scientific knowledge. These and other questions will haunt the gatekeeper's lodge for some time to come, and it may be that there is no easy answer to them. However, it would appear that there is an appetite developing, at common law in Scotland, to scrutinise the credentials of witnesses as well as the nature of the science and craft claimed as expertise, before allowing the evidence further passage into the arena of proof. A good example of this more robust approach occurred in a reference to the appeal court by the Scottish Criminal Case Review Commission. In that case, a novel forensic method of excluding a suspect, pioneered by the FBI, called case linkage analysis (CLA) was held insufficiently rigorous to pass a reliability test of admissibility applied by the court. This is the first occasion this test has been formulated and represents a material development of the common law. The criminal appeal court said:

> [54] Evidence about relevant matters which are not within the knowledge of everyday life reasonably to be imputed to a jury or other finder of fact may be admissible if it is likely to assist the jury or finder of fact in the proper determination of the issue before it. The expert evidence must be relevant to that issue (and so not concerned solely with collateral issues), and it must be based on a recognised and developed academic discipline. It must proceed on theories which have been tested (both by academic review and in practice) and found to have a practical and measurable consequence in real life. It must follow a developed methodology which is explicable and open to possible challenge, and it must produce a result which is capable of being assessed and given more or less weight in light of all the evidence before the finder of fact. If the evidence does not meet these criteria, it will not assist the finder of fact in the proper determination of the issue; rather, it will risk confusing or distracting the finder of fact, or, worse still, cause the finder of fact to determine the crucial issue on the basis of unreliable or erroneous evidence. For this reason, the court will not admit evidence from a "man of skill" or an "expert" unless satisfied that the evidence is sufficiently reliable that it will assist the finder of fact in the proper determination of the issue before it.
>
> (***Young v HM Advocate***)[13]

This 'enhanced' threshold reliability test for determining the admissibility of expert evidence appears to be in six parts. Some aspects of the test are new. Some aspects are long established. Now, for expert opinion evidence to be admitted to probation necessity, relevance and materiality alone are insufficient. The expert testimony must satisfy further criteria:

1. It must be necessary to assist the jury and not something which is within reasonable contemplation or knowledge of the average juror.
2. It must be relevant and not collateral.
3. It must be based on recognised and established principles.
4. It must proceed on theories which have been tested and are quantifiable.
5. It must follow a developed methodology; be inherently consistent, coherent and susceptible to contradiction or challenge.
6. It must be accessible and assessable.

Scientists and other experts will doubtless argue that the language used in the test raises as many questions as it answers. I showed the test to two eminent scientists in Scotland, both of whom spent the next hour arguing about what it means. Where this test and the language used in it came from is not clear from the judgement. As a test of admissibility, it might be thought to favour those areas of expertise which are already established and are, unlike the 'soft sciences', more gravitationally aligned to empirical research, experiment and quantification. What is a 'developed methodology' in the context of science? Who determines when a body of knowledge can be said to be 'a developed methodology'? By what criteria is that issue measured? The meaning of developed methodology is unexplained. As a legal test, it seems clearly weighted in favour of orthodoxy rather than new or emerging science or expertise. In that sense it is a 'scientific community'–based test, but it will be for the gateway judges to be satisfied that the proffered expert testimony passes the test. The language of the test resonates with that used by the U.S. Supreme Court in *Daubert v Merrell Dow Pharmaceuticals Inc*[14] and its Canadian Supreme Court counterpart *R v J-L.*[15] *Daubert* introduced a non-exclusive four-factor enhanced admissibility test for judges in the United States to determine the admissibility of expert opinion evidence. The four factors which must be identified and established in a pre-proof chamber by a judge exercising a gatekeeper function are:

1. Has the theory or technique been tested? 'Scientific methodology today is based on generating hypotheses and testing them to see if they can be falsified; indeed, this methodology is what distinguishes science from other fields of human inquiry'.[16]
2. Has it been subject to peer review and publication? 'Submission to the scrutiny of the scientific community is a component of "good science", in part because it increases the likelihood that substantive flaws in methodology will be detected'.[17]
3. Does it enjoy general scientific acceptance? 'A reliability assessment does not require, although it does permit, explicit identification of a relevant scientific community and an express determination of a particular degree of acceptance within that community. ... Widespread acceptance can be an important factor in ruling particular evidence admissible, and "a known technique which has been able to attract only minimal support within the community," ... may properly be viewed with skepticism'.[18]
4. Is there an error rate to measure confidence and are there standards controlling its operation?

The language and concepts expressed in the *Daubert* test are very similar to those found in *Young*. A *caveat* might be noted about *Daubert*. The confidence the court expressed in the majority, that federal district judges would be able to man the gate appropriately, was not shared by the then chief justice (Rehnquist), who uncharacteristically dissented with the following observation about the potential danger inherent in allowing predominantly scientifically untutored judges, to assess scientific and quasi-scientific theories for methodological rigour and validity using the *Daubert* model of admissibility test:

> I defer to no one in my confidence in federal judges; but I am at a loss to know what is meant when it is said that the scientific status of a theory depends on its "falsifiability," and I suspect some of them will be, too. I do not doubt that [the relevant US Rule] confides to the judge some gatekeeping responsibility in deciding questions of the admissibility of proffered expert testimony. But I do not think it imposes on them either the obligation or the authority to become amateur scientists in order to perform that role.

The same question arises in Scotland. Does the contemporary judiciary possess the insight and scientific skill needed to assess and evaluate the status of a new or complex scientific theory and methodology?

2.4 Extra Judicial Inquiry

The Scottish Law Commission has not published in this area. However, serious concern developed in England and Wales following a series of well-known miscarriage cases which had as their focus the failure of the forensic process in the courtroom.[19] An inquiry ensued and the Law Commission, following a wide consultation,[20] recommended to Parliament in a 2011 report, 'Expert Evidence in Criminal Proceedings in England and Wales' (Law Com No. 325), that an admissibility test for expert testimony ought to be introduced by primary legislation. A principal concern of the Law Commission was the ease with which certain expert evidence could be admitted into the trial process without the sufficiently proper and robust scrutiny of an admissibility or reliability test. By March 2013, the House of Commons Science and Technology Committee (again) called for a long-awaited government response to the 2011 recommendation of the Law Commission. The committee said: 'The Government has had two years to respond to the Law Commission's proposals for an admissibility test for expert evidence and should publish its response without further delay. We recommend that the Government supports the Law Commission's proposals'. The rather shortsighted and disappointing government response, rejecting the need for primary legislation on cost grounds, eventually appeared in November 2013:[21]

> The Government shares the Law Commission's concern about problems caused by the use of inappropriate or unreliable expert evidence, and is persuaded of the benefits of taking action on this. It recognises the potential value of the proposed reliability test in reducing the risk of unsafe convictions arising from unreliable expert evidence. However, there is no robust estimate of the size of the problem to be tackled – either in terms of the number of cases

> where unreliable expert evidence is adduced, nor in the impact this has in terms of subsequently quashed convictions. The impact assessment published with the Law Commission's recommendations indicates that application of the new test would involve additional pre-trial hearings, with the concomitant additional costs, but without sufficient reliably predictable savings to compensate for those costs. Without certainty as to the offsetting savings which might be achieved, when set against current resource constraints it is not feasible to implement the proposals in full at this time.

Instead, in England and Wales, the Criminal Procedure Rules were revised to adopt as many of the Law Commission recommendations as possible to introduce by court rule what cannot be introduced by statute. Civil Practice Directions were also issued.

Concern has not evaporated on the back of these limited reforms. Thus, in a case about false memory syndrome (*R v H*)[22] Lord Justice Leveson PQBD said:

> Before leaving an examination of the principles governing admissibility of this type of evidence, it is appropriate to note the general concern about expert witnesses. Whilst legislative reform has not been taken forward, following the Law Commission Report on Expert Evidence in Criminal Proceedings, there is real concern about the use of unreliable or inappropriate expert evidence. As a result, Part 33 of the Criminal Procedure Rules has been revised (with effect from 1 October 2014) and a new Practice Direction[23] is to be published which will incorporate the reliability factors recommended by the Law Commission for the admission of expert evidence.

Rule 33 of the Criminal Procedure Rules 2014/1610 now regulates the way in which an expert's evidence can be introduced in evidence. The rule includes an overriding objective which repeats the common law admissibility test and sets out the matters an expert's written report should cover:

2.4.1 Content of Expert's Report

Where rule 33.3(3) applies, an expert's report must—

- (a) give details of the expert's qualifications, relevant experience and accreditation;
- (b) give details of any literature or other information which the expert has relied on in making the report;
- (c) contain a statement setting out the substance of all facts given to the expert which are material to the opinions expressed in the report, or upon which those opinions are based;
- (d) make clear which of the facts stated in the report are within the expert's own knowledge;

(e) say who carried out any examination, measurement, test or experiment which the expert has used for the report and—
  (i) give the qualifications, relevant experience and accreditation of that person,
  (ii) say whether or not the examination, measurement, test or experiment was carried out under the expert's supervision, and
  (iii) summarise the findings on which the expert relies;
(f) where there is a range of opinion on the matters dealt with in the report—
  (i) summarise the range of opinion, and
  (ii) give reasons for the expert's own opinion;
(g) if the expert is not able to give an opinion without qualification, state the qualification;
(h) include such information as the court may need to decide whether the expert's opinion is sufficiently reliable to be admissible as evidence;
(i) contain a summary of the conclusions reached;
(j) contain a statement that the expert understands an expert's duty to the court, and has complied and will continue to comply with that duty; and
(k) contain the same declaration of truth as a witness statement.

The Practice Direction for civil procedure is in similar terms. A material failure to conform with the rules or Practice Direction could theoretically render the expert's opinion inadmissible. This *ad hoc* and limited regulatory structure falls far short of the Law Commission's vision to introduce an admissibility test.

2.5 Conclusion

In both Scotland and England and Wales, there is an acute awareness of the need to manage the inappropriate use of expert testimony. The response to the difficulties encountered in both jurisdictions has been different. In Scotland the common law has been tentatively developed to introduce a more rigorous admissibility test. In England and Wales, a more systematic reform recommended by the Law Commission has been rejected by government leaving it to the judicial authorities to self-regulate using and adapting court rules and directions to achieve this purpose. In neither jurisdiction is the answer to the challenges posed by new and more complex science in court satisfactory. Both jurisdictions have for different reasons opted for piecemeal and arguably inadequate reform rather than root and branch holistic change. In both instances the net result is unsatisfactory.

Acknowledgement

My thanks to Steven Balmer, solicitor, for his assistance with research for this chapter.

Notes

1. 1953 S.C. 34.
2. See also *Dingley v Chief Constable, Strathclyde Police* 2000 SC (HL) 77, 1998 SC 548 at 555; *McTear v Imperial Tobacco Ltd (No 1)* 2005 2 S.C. 1.
3. In a very small class of cases the ultimate judicial issue may be so finely balanced as to come down solely to which, of competing opinions, is to be preferred. Only then could the expert opinion be said to be truly dispositive, if preferred.
4. 509 U.S. 579 (1993).
5. See *National Justice Campania Naviera, SA v Prudential Assurance Co. Ltd ('The Ikarion Reefer')* (1993) 2 Lloyd's Rep. 68 per Cresswell J and the duties of an expert to express an opinion professionally and with restraint.
6. 2009 J.C. 336; 2009 S.C.L. 1047.
7. Ibid.
8. See also *Pierce v HM Advocate* 1981 SCLR 783 where an expert was criticised for omitting from his oral testimony material contained in his report: 'This was in our judgment, conduct on the part of an expert witness which demonstrated a complete misunderstanding of the role of scientific witnesses in the Courts, and a lack of the essential qualities of accuracy and scientific objectivity which are normally to be taken for granted'. LJG Emslie.
9. Criminal Justice and Licensing (Scotland) Act 2010 s.121; Renton and Brown Criminal Procedure (6th edition), Chapter 13A – Disclosure; see also Criminal Procedure (Scotland) Act 1995 s.70A(9) for defence duty to disclose.
10. U.S. and Canada, for example.
11. Fn 6 ibid.
12. *Kennedy v Cordia (Services) LLP* 2014 S.L.T. 984; 2014 Rep. L.R. 127.
13. (2013) HCJAC 145; 2014 S.C.L. 98.
14. 509 U.S. 579 (1993).
15. (2000) 2 SCR 600; see generally 'Wrongful Convictions and the Magical Aura of the Courtroom', I Binnie Juridical Review (2011) 10 TJR 141.
16. *Daubert* at 593.
17. Ibid.
18. Ibid. at 594.
19. See *R v Dallagher* (2002) EWCA Crim 1903; *R v Clark* (2003) EWCA Crim 1020; *R v Cannings* (2004) EWCA Crim 1; *R v Harris* and others (2005) EWCA Crim 1980.
20. 'The admissibility of expert evidence in criminal proceedings in England and Wales' Consultation Paper No. 190 (2009–2010).
21. The government's response to the Law Commission report: *Expert Evidence in Criminal Proceedings in England and Wales* (Law Com No. 325) 21 November 2013
22. (2014) Crim. L.R. 905.
23. Practice Direction 35.

Miscarriages of Justice and the Role of the Expert Witness

3

LUCINA HACKMAN

Contents

3.1 Introduction

Miscarriages of justice have had an impact on the role of the expert witness and the way in which the expert must act within the legal jurisdictions of the UK.

Various causes of miscarriages of justice have been identified and discussed (Naughton 2004; Walker and McCartney 2008), but arguably those that draw the greatest amount of high-profile attention involve the mismanagement of expert evidence and are related to the actions of the expert witness or witnesses. These cases take on an infamy of their own and lead to huge media attention, often leading to subsequent inquiries, reports and recommendations (The Law Commission 2011; May 1994; Runciman and May 1993).

While the term 'miscarriage of justice' has slightly different meanings for different groups, Nobles and Schiff (2000) identify two principal components present in all cases 'the people who have been convicted of the offences did not in fact commit those offences, or that their convictions were flawed because some part of the process that produced those convictions did not operate as it should'. A miscarriage of justice can also only be identified in retrospect since it is not until a case is presented to, and determined upon, by aCourt of Appeal that a decision is made that the miscarriage of justice has occurred (Naughton 2004). Until a Court of Appeal has examined the case and quashed the conviction, the miscarriage of justice can only ever be alleged, although this does not prevent the media from hypothesising in these cases (Nobles and Schiff 1995). Indeed, there are a number of occasions when pressure which has originated within the media has pushed forward a case, bringing it to the attention of the public and giving momentum to the subsequent appeal process (Gies 2016; Savage et al. 2007; Warden 2001). Once completed, a successful appeal indicates that a wrongful conviction has occurred and therefore there has been some failure in the prosecution process (Nobles and Schiff 1995; Walker 1999). A detailed discussion of the causes of miscarriages of justice is beyond the remit of this chapter; however, the role that expert witnesses have played within the identified miscarriages of justice will be examined. It should also be noted that while a small number of miscarriages of justice become headline news and part of the popularist discourse, there a greater number of convictions that are successfully overturned through routine appellate procedures that are never heard of by the general public (Naughton 2003, 2004, 2007).

The role of the expert witness in the different courts of the countries that make up the UK therefore can experience high-profile scrutiny. This scrutiny is often brought into greater focus by the part that the expert witness and their expert evidence has played in a number of miscarriages of justice. Issues associated with the role of the expert witness were exposed by the appeals into the Birmingham Six[1] and child death cases of Sally Clarke[2] and Angela Canning,[3] which were widely discussed in the media. The added potential for expert witness evidence to cause miscarriages of justice has become identified in the UK, due to the media attention that these cases garner, and as a result of initiatives such as the Innocence Project in the United States.[4] A quick examination of the literature emphasises that miscarriages of justice are not limited to any one country or any one justice system (Cooley and Turvey 2014; Sangha et al. 2010). How often they occur, however, is more difficult to determine since many cases do not go to appeal and the work of groups such as the Innocence Project are limited to cases where biological material survives and can be retested with the results being utilised as the basis of the appeal process (Medwed 2002). These exonerations have, however, allowed an analysis of the cases that have been successfully appealed in order to identify the causes for the initial miscarriage (Garrett and Neufeld 2009). There are a number of common themes which emerge from this analysis, including issues with eyewitness testimony; most importantly, more than 50% of the wrongful convictions involved invalid or erroneous expert forensic evidence (Garret and Neufeld 2009). A similar study by Langdon and Wilson (2005) in which 32 cases from Australia and New Zealand were analysed, demonstrated many parallels to the issues which were found by the work of Garret and Neufeld (2009). The role of the expert witness and forensic science in these miscarriages of justice becomes inescapable.

While most of the cases discussed here will be based on appeals which have been heard in courts of the UK, including those of England and Wales, Scotland and Northern Ireland, the issues that are raised are internationally relevant. This chapter examines the role of the expert witness and the ways in which it has been both informed and formed by these high-profile miscarriages of justice.

3.2 The Role of the Expert Witness

The expert witness is alone in the courtroom in being able to give opinion evidence and is there to assist the court with elucidating and presenting information about a specialist subject which is outside the expertise of the jury[5] (Ward 2015). This anomalous role was developed during the eighteenth century and the ability to give an opinion remains the primary factor that separates the role of the expert witness from that of other witnesses in court (Rix 1999). The history and development of the role has not been without controversy from the beginning of its development to the present day. The introduction of scientific expertise to the courtroom carries the expectation that the science put before the court will provide clear and unequivocal answers to questions posed (Mnookin 2007). This view is underpinned with an expectation that science itself is a process that produces 'infallible truth' and carries with it certainty which is understood by those on the receiving end of the testimony to mean that through the application of scientific methodology and experiment a problem will be solved and explained (Golan 1999). This cultural understanding of science is carried into the courtroom by those who make up the court, including the judiciary and members of the jury (Golan 1999; Mnookin 2007). This ability to supply the 'answer' or solve a problem does not always prove to be the case, as scientists have been and continue to be shown to be unable to provide the answers requested and in many cases may often not agree on the same conclusion given the same evidence to examine (Golan 1999; Mnookin 2007).

The role of the scientifically knowledgeable expert who presents an opinion about the facts has always invited scrutiny, especially since the role itself, as it is situated within the adversarial system, invites conflict. This is no more apparent than when opposing scientific experts are introduced to give their interpretation of the facts that are in question (Mason 1986; Mnookin 2007; Redmayne 1996; Vidmar and Diamond 2000). This has thrown into relief the reality that despite the theory of the existence of a single scientific truth, there are often a number of opinions which can be presented to the court, leading eventually to frustrations for the court itself (Redmayne 1996). This lack of agreement on the science between experts, such as those found in relation to the shaken baby syndrome controversy, can cause enormous issues for the courts and has led to frustration by the courts as well as expert witnesses which has impacted the justice process as well as the lives of those involved, be they the expert witness, the judges or the accused (Golan 1999; Tuerkheimer 2009). For the expert witness, being caught in these controversies can be professionally detrimental. In 2016, Dr Wendy Squiers was taken before a General Medical Council (GMC) tribunal in relation to her evidence in cases of shaken baby syndrome (SBS), also known as non-accidental head injury (NAHI). Her presence in front of the tribunal was centred solely upon her appearance as an expert in court and the evidence that she had presented in six cases. She was accused of failing to act within her area of expertise, failing to be objective and unbiased and being 'deliberately misleading'.[6] Dr Squiers was initially struck off the GMC medical register in March 2016 only to be reinstated in November of the same year, although she remains unable to give evidence as an expert witness in criminal, civil or family courts.[7] She was reinstated because at issue was not her expertise in her medical field but her actions as an expert witness.

In the UK, the publication and recommendations of many of the inquiries that have come about because of these high-profile miscarriages of justice have resulted in legislation and guidelines which the expert must adhere to when they are working within the legal arena.[8,9] What is apparent when examining the developments and changes which have influenced the role and actions of the expert witness, however, is that these are not static and there are constant developments and challenges to the role of the expert witness.

3.3 Disclosure of Evidence

The appeals of the Birmingham Six,[10] Maguire Seven[11] and Judith Ward[12] were all examples in which the Court of Appeal exposed issues with forensic science processes and the disclosure of evidence by expert witnesses.

The Birmingham Six comprised six individuals who were convicted of setting bombs in Birmingham which killed 21 people and injured a further 162 others.[13] Forensic evidence presented at the trial identified that all of the accused had tested positive for nitroglycerin on their hands which, it was argued, suggested that they had recently handled explosives (Walker and Stockdale 1995). Despite unsuccessful appeals, a book by investigative journalist Chris Mullin (1997) raised enough concerns about the scientific evidence that had been presented on court, to cause the home secretary to refer the case again to the Court of Appeal in 1987, although it wasn't until a further Court of Appeal hearing in 1991 that they were finally exonerated of all charges (Sangha et al. 2010). The Court of Appeal in 1987 found that there were issues with tests employed by the investigating scientist, Dr Skuse (Schurr 1993). These tests were used to examine swabs taken from the hands of the suspects. The Court of Appeal established that the test that was finally relied upon in court was not specific for nitroglycerin.[14] It also discounted the possibility of contamination; however, the 1991 appeal had access to evidence which demonstrated that the tests utilised in the original investigation could give false positives. This led the Court of Appeal to state that the conclusions drawn by Dr Skuse were 'wrong, demonstrably wrong, judged even by the state of forensic science in 1974'.[15]

The Maguire Seven were convicted, alongside a group known as the Guildford Four, of the Guildford pub bombings of 5 October 1974. The convictions of the Guildford Four were quashed in 1989 on grounds of police misconduct; a public inquiry was set up by the home secretary to identify if there had been potential problems with how scientific evidence was handled during the case against the Maguire Seven. This public inquiry, known as the May Inquiry, concentrated on the issues that were identified in relation to the forensic science that had been used in the Guildford Four and Maguire Seven inquiries, and found that the blame for errors and mistakes lay mainly with the forensic scientists (May 1994). As a result of this inquiry, the case was referred to the Court of Appeal, which in turn quashed their convictions. The scientific evidence against the Maguire Seven centred on the discovery of the presence of nitroglycerin on the hands and/or gloves of the accused. The trial scientists argued that there was no innocent explanation for the presence of the nitroglycerin other than through handling explosive material (Sangha et al. 2010) The May Inquiry consulted an analytical chemist, Professor Thorburn Burns, who demonstrated by experiments that contamination was in fact a possibility (Sangha et al. 2010; Schurr 1993).

The investigation led by Sir John May demonstrated that there were irregularities with the scientific evidence, that the scientists had been selective about the tests and data that they had produced, and that they had chosen to present and disclose those tests and test results that supported their case, ignoring those that did not (May 1994). This demonstrated a non-partisanship approach to the investigation. Additionally, there were a number of tests which were performed but which were not disclosed prior to or during the trail.[16] The non-disclosure of information that had been exposed during the inquiry was addressed in the appeal, which quashed the original sentence: 'We are of the opinion that a forensic scientist who is an adviser to the prosecuting authority is under a duty to disclose material of which he knows and which may have "some bearing on the offence charged and the surrounding circumstances of the case". The disclosure will be to the authority which retains him and which must in turn (subject to sensitivity) disclose the information to the defence. We hold that there is such a duty because we can see no cause to distinguish between members of the prosecuting authority and those advising it in the capacity of a forensic scientist'.[16]

The referral of Judith Ward's[17] case to the Court of Appeal followed closely after this successful appeal since once again, scientific evidence identifying nitroglycerin on Judith Ward's hands was central to the prosecution case. Judith Ward had been convicted of setting bombs which had resulted in the death of 12 people in 1974. The previous inquiries and appeals had shed doubt on the scientific evidence, and this last appeal proved that the case suffered from similar issues, including a lack of disclosure by the scientists. The Court of Appeal described the disclosure of evidence as 'woefully deficient'. They stated that 'an incident of the right to a fair trial is a right to timely disclosure by the prosecution of all material matters which affect the scientific case relied on by the prosecution. This duty exists whether or not a specific request for disclosure of details of scientific evidence is made by the defence. The duty is continuous'.[18] As with the Maguire Seven, the science and the scientists were described as lacking and presenting a distorted picture to the court.

The Runciman Royal Commission Inquiry was also set up as a result of these identified miscarriages of justice (Runciman and May 1993). This inquiry examined a number of failings in relation to forensic science and the ways in which it was presented in court, including requirements for disclosure, the need for both prosecution and defence to have the same access to resources, the need for scientists to maintain impartiality and objectivity, the requirement for proficiency testing, prosecution bias and the failure to interpret evidence and communicate findings appropriately. Of interest was the call for forensic scientists to be externally audited and to have a code of practice to which they must adhere. These calls to regulate crime laboratories and the forensic scientists that work within them have been reiterated again and again in reports and inquiries (National Research Council 2009; President's Council of Advisors on Science and Technology 2016). It was as a result of the May and Runciman Inquiries that the Criminal Cases Review Commission (CRCC) was established. This describes itself as having been set up to 'take a fresh, independent look at suspected miscarriages of justice in England, Wales and Northern Ireland'.[19]

There were further failures of disclosure exposed during the appeal against conviction by Sally Clark. While her first appeal upheld the original conviction, a second appeal was successful when it emerged that Dr Alan Williams, the home office pathologist who undertook the examinations of both of her children, had failed to disclose all of the tests and reports, especially the microbiological reports which suggested that Harry, her second son, could have died of natural circumstances. This test had revealed the presence of *Staphylococcus aureus* bacteria, providing the possibility that he died of acute infection or inflammation.[20]

Sally Clark was accused of causing the death of both of her sons after her second son, Harry, died. The circumstances of both deaths were very similar, both having happened suddenly while the babies were young. Christopher was 11 weeks old and Harry was 8 weeks old. When Christopher died, his body was examined by Dr Alan Williams, who observed bruises on the body and a small split to the frenulum which he concluded were consistent with attempts at resuscitation. There was evidence of infection in the lungs, and therefore cause of death was concluded to be lower respiratory tract infection and the death treated as a case of sudden infant death syndrome (SIDS). The death of Harry happened in 1998, and again the body was examined by Dr Alan Williams. In this case, Dr Williams found injuries which he linked to repeated episodes of shaking, and therefore this shaking was the likely cause of death. This second death and associated conclusion caused Dr Williams to look back at the death of Christopher and re-examine the retained material from that postmortem, which included photographs and slides from the lungs. Thereafter, he changed his opinion on the first death and concluded that it too had been unnatural and that there was evidence of smothering.[21] This resulted in the arrest of Sally Clark and her husband and her eventual conviction for causing harm to her sons.

In 2000, a first appeal was heard and the original conviction upheld; however, subsequent to this appeal records of microbiological tests on samples gathered during the postmortem of Harry by Dr Williams were discovered. These tests and their results were known to Dr Williams, and they showed that *Staphylococcus aureus* bacteria were present in the lungs, stomach tissue and cerebrospinal fluid when Harry died.[22] The case was referred back to the Court of Appeal by the Criminal Cases Review Commission for further scrutiny. The Court of Appeal finally came to the conclusion that 'since there was evidence that was not before the jury that might have caused the jury to reach a different verdict on the count in respect of Harry; the verdict on that count has in our judgement to be viewed as unsafe and must be quashed'.[22]

It was clear to the Appeal Court that Dr Williams had known about both the tests and their results; however, none of his statements, of which there were three, included any mention of them in relation to Harry. During examination in chief he also neglected to mention that he had taken the samples or that he had submitted them for testing, although he did make the tests undertaken on Christopher available for the medical experts. Dr Williams was given a number of chances when giving his oral evidence in court to discuss any samples and test undertaken on Harry and did not avail himself of these. Dr Williams never gave a statement about why he did not disclose the tests or their results except to state that 'it is not in my practice to refer to additional results in my post mortem unless they are relevant to the cause of death, as the specimens were referred to another consultant'. The Court of Appeal found that this explanation was 'wholly unacceptable' since it was out of line with the standard practice of other pathologists, likely to mislead others, finding that 'it runs a significant risk of a miscarriage of justice. It is tantamount to saying "If I can discount it, nobody else need consider it". As an approach it only has to be voiced for the inherent danger to be obvious'.[22]

In relation to the issues surrounding the lack of disclosure by Dr Williams the Appeal Court highlighted two responsibilities of expert witnesses. First, they should undertake their investigations to an acceptable standard. The Appeal Court acknowledged that the first investigation creates change in the evidence. This means that any following expert has to rely to an extent on the accurate and high standard work of the first expert; this includes accurate recording of activities, tests, results and examinations, whether the results are negative or not and whether or not they support the hypothesis that the expert has developed. In relation to paediatric postmortems in the UK this case and its subsequent appeals together with the similar cases which also came before the Court of Appeal as a result of this case were the driver for the development of a set of protocols developed by Baroness Kennedy on behalf of the Royal College of Pathologists and the Royal College of Paediatrics and Child Health for the investigation of sudden unexpected death in infancy.[23] This includes the requirement that all tests, no matter whether they cast doubt on the formed opinion, should be disclosed.

The requirement for disclosure was reiterated by a document published as a result of the attorney general's investigation into cases involving shaken baby prosecutions in 2006 called 'Disclosure: Expert's Evidence and Unused Material'. This document, which was updated in 2010,[24] outlines the role and responsibilities of the expert in relation to the evidence that they accrue and which they have in their possession. In summary, it is the responsibility of the expert to record everything in a durable and retrievable form, to retain this material until such times as they are instructed to discard or destroy anything and to reveal it when this is requested for disclosure, often shortened to record, retain, reveal. The obligation by the prosecution team to disclose is outlined in the Criminal Procedure and Investigations Act 1996.[25] As outlined in the 'Disclosure: Expert's Evidence and Unused Material' document, the expert must make the prosecution team aware of all material that they have, thereby 'assisting in ensuring that the Prosecution Team can comply fully with their statutory disclosure obligations'.[26] The guide identifies the material covered by the disclosure rules 'during the course of any investigation material is generated. Some of it is used as evidence and other material is not used. The material that is not used as evidence is known as unused material, to which the disclosure regime applies'.[27] The guide goes on to define unused material as 'material that is relevant to the investigation but which does not actually form part of the case for the prosecution against the accused. Even though the material may not be used as evidence, it is important that for the purposes of disclosure this material is retained. It is not for you to determine whether the material generated in the course of an investigation is relevant to the investigation'.[27] This obligates the expert to keep and disclose material which allows the prosecution team to fulfil their obligations in turn. Thus, materials which might be relevant to the defendant's case should be disclosed according to the 'golden rule' of disclosure defined in *R v C&H* by Lord Bingham,[27] who stated that 'fairness ordinarily requires that any material held by the prosecution which weakens its case or strengthens that of the defendant, if not relied on as part of its formal case against the defendant should be disclosed to the defence'. The disclosure guide removes the requirement for the expert to decide what is relevant and instead the expert is required to compile an index of *all* unused material that can then be passed on. Case law subsequent to the Clark appeal has indicated that all unused material should be examined by the defence.[28]

3.4 Impartiality and Bias

In addition to the issue of non-disclosure, the appeals into the Maguire Seven, Birmingham Six and Judith Ward all exposed the problem of bias in relation to the evidence given by the expert witnesses. The experts were accused of having lost their impartiality. In the case of Judith Ward, the Court of Appeal stated, 'Forensic scientists may become partisan. The very fact that the police seek their assistance may create a relationship between the police and the forensic scientists. And the adversarial character of the proceedings tend to promote this process. Forensic scientists employed by the government may come to see their function as helping the police. They may lose their objectivity'.[29] The court went on to conclude, 'First we have identified the cause of the case as stemming from the fact that three senior forensic scientists at RARDE regarded their risk as being to help the police. They became partisan. It is the clear duty of government forensic scientists to assist in a neutral and impartial way in criminal investigations. They must act in the cause of justice. That duty should be spelt out to all engaged in forensic services in the clearest terms'.[30]

In addition to the issues related to disclosure, the Runciman Royal Commission report[30] recognised the need for forensic scientists to take a more balanced approach to their work to ensure that they remain impartial and unbiased (Runciman and May 1993). To achieve this, they suggested that an issue was that the provision of forensic science was undertaken by a limited number of public sector laboratories, restricting the access to forensic services by the defence. They recommended that these laboratories undertake work for the defence as well as the prosecution and that their work be subject to external audit. An increase in research which was based in centres of excellence, including universities as well as in the public sector, was also called for as the report recognised the role that research played in the development of standards and practices. The Runciman Royal

Commission also noted that while codes of practice for forensic science had been drafted, there were potential issues surrounding the ability to enforce them, so it recommended the formation of an oversight body such as a forensic science advisory council that could create codes of practice for forensic scientists which would cover their professional responsibilities, including codes of ethics and disclosure responsibilities; 'if such as code were applied to all forensic scientists, including those in the private sector, the new Council might be given regulatory powers itself or asked to recommend how such a code should be enforced in some other way. In addition to these responsibilities for codes of practice and the regulation of the profession, we envisage that the new Council should keep under review the arrangements for the training of forensic scientists and their assistance and the means by which they are kept up to date with the latest scientific discoveries' (Runciman and May 1993).

It was not until 2008 that a forensic regulator was appointed in England and Wales and these codes of practice began to be developed. The forensic regulator has written a general code of practice[31] as well as guides relating to subjects such as bias,[32] contamination[33] and validation.[34] In addition to the general code, there are also subject-specific codes which have been published for identified subject areas such as forensic anthropology.[35]

In addition to these changes, there has also been an increase in research to investigate the sources of bias that could have an impact on forensic scientists and their decision making (Budowle et al. 2009; Dror and Hampikian 2011; Miller 1984, 1987). This research has concentrated on demonstrating where bias can affect the final decision of the forensic scientist and therefore ways in which it can then be avoided or at least mitigated against. This research has been further fuelled by inquiries such as the Fingerprint Inquiry in Scotland.[36] This inquiry came about as a direct result of the identification and verification of fingerprints associated with *HM Advocate v McKie*.[37] During a murder investigation, a finger mark was recovered from within the house of the victim that was identified as originating from Shirley McKie, at that time a serving police officer. She denied having entered the locus and therefore that the fingerprint was hers. As a result of this denial she was suspended, sacked and eventually arrested for perjury, having stated in court, while giving evidence, that she had not entered the building. A jury found her not guilty of perjury, but Ms McKie sued her former employers for the manner of her arrest. Eventually, there was an out-of-court settlement with Ms McKie and an inquiry was launched to investigate the events surrounding the identification of the fingerprint.[38] This, as well as other high-profile issues with fingerprint matching, such as the misidentification of a fingerprint by the FBI in the Mayfield affair (OIG 2006), is an example of confirmation bias that can be shown to influence the conclusions that an expert witness might draw from evidence.

3.5 Evaluation and Presentation of Evidence

In 2010, the Court of Appeal delivered a judgement on the case of *R v T*.[39] T had been convicted of murder and the identification of his presence at the scene was at the core of his appeal. That identification included the analysis of footwear marks which had been recovered from the crime scene and their comparison with Nike trainers found at the defendant's house after his arrest. As part of the matching process the forensic scientist used a series of databases to create a statistical probability that the footwear mark was made by the pair of Nike shoes which had been seized. His calculations took into account the pattern of the prints, the size of the shoe as far as it could be determined and the wear on the shoes and any discrepancies between the patterns of the print recovered from the scene and those of the recovered trainers. From these he calculated the likelihood ratio that the shoes had made the recovered prints; this likelihood ratio was an attempt to give a more standardised form to his results (Redmayne et al. 2011). However, none of the calculations that he undertook or the assumptions that he had made during the process of calculating the likelihood ratio were included in his report. He also did not refer to it in his testimony when he gave evidence; instead, he translated the figures created into a verbal scale. This verbal scale was being used at the time by the Forensic Science Service and provided a verbal equivalent to likelihood rations which ranged from weak when the likelihood ratio was >1–10 through to extremely strong support when it was >1,000,000. In this case the likelihood ratios translated to moderate (Redmayne et al. 2011). He presented his conclusion to the court as 'in my opinion there is a moderate degree of scientific support for the view that [the Nike trainers] made those marks'.[40]

The results of the *R v T*[41] appeal were long awaited by forensic scientists in the UK because of the use of Bayesian statistics and the likelihood ratio, which had already been rejected by the Court of Appeal for non-DNA evidence types.[42] Within their response, the Court of Appeal challenged the use of both of these methods for the development of forensic probabilities for court. The use of statistics in the courtroom is discussed elsewhere in this book and so will not be repeated here; however, of note are the remarks by the Court of Appeal in relation to the way that the evidence was presented. The written report is one of the two methods of communication that are available to the expert witness and are part of the requirements of the role. An expert witness provides a written report for the court which contains their actions, opinions and conclusions. In an effort to remove the issue of the expert as advocate, the report, as with the presentation of evidence at court, is aimed at the court itself as an end user. Each report can be disclosed and allows the advocates to introduce the expert evidence that will be presented in court. While the expert may then be called upon to give evidence in the courtroom, this may not be the case and the opinion within the report may be simply accepted by both sides. In the case of *R v T*, the Court of Appeal pointed out, 'In … reports for the trial … there was no reference at all to any of these statistics, the formula or to the use of a likelihood ratio or to the scale of numerical values set out. … The conclusion in his first report, which was supported by the statistics, formula and resulting likelihood ratio, was expressed solely in terms of the verbal scale'.[43] The Court of Appeal notes that as a result of not including the information about methodologies within the report, the expert was then not challenged within the courtroom when he gave evidence. As they stressed, expert reports should be transparent, should include any evidence on which the expert's opinion is based and should allow those who examine it to follow their reasoning. None of this should be omitted, even if it might have the potential to confuse the jury. The Court of Appeal felt that this approach obscured the way in which the expert reached his opinion and therefore was not transparent; indeed, some authors have reported that the court identified a complete failure of transparency (Redmayne et al. 2011). This lack of transparency did not conform to the legislative requirements that go as far back as *Davie v Edinburgh Magistrates*,[44] where the duty of the expert is to 'furnish the … jury with the necessary scientific criteria for testing the accuracy of their conclusions'. This is also recognised in modern legislative requirements for the expert, including the Criminal Procedure Rules, which states that the expert must 'give details of any literature or other information which the expert has relied on in making the report'.[45] While it could be argued that in fact full transparency is an ideal rather than a fact since it would not be possible to include absolutely all reading, thought processes and conversations that have gone into forming any opinion into any given report, the forensic scientist is able to decide what information is important and pertinent to the case and ensure that it is included (Hamer 2012). It does remain the case, underlined by the events of *R v T*, that all reasoning and investigation should be explained as clearly and fully as possible by the expert within their report. This should be presented in such a way that both peer reviewer and anyone else reading the report should understand the arguments and thought processes well enough that they can challenge them if appropriate.

3.6 Reliability of Expert Evidence

In 1996 Dorothy Wood was murdered by an intruder who had forced a window in her bedroom and suffocated her with a pillow. During the examination of the scene, ear prints were recovered from the glass of the window. This same window had been cleaned 2–3 weeks previously and was located below the window that had been forced open to effect entry to the property. Subsequently in 1998 Mark Dallagher[46] was convicted of the murder of Mrs Wood. At trial, evidence upon which most emphasis was placed was that of an ear print found at the scene which was ascertained to be a match to comparison prints of Mark Dallagher's ear by two expert witnesses (Halpin 2008; Morris 2008).

There were a number of sections to the appeal against this conviction, all of which centred on the ear print evidence. It was of note that while no experts had been presented to the court by the defence at the time of the trial in relation to the ear print evidence, shortly after the trial concluded there was a publication in a peer-reviewed journal which questioned the reliability of ear prints as an individualising evidence type (Champod et al. 2001). The admissibility of the ear print evidence was examined by the Appeal Court as well as the way in which the evidence was presented by the experts; it was argued that they had committed the prosecutor's fallacy by presenting the evidence in such a way that it was too favourable to the prosecution and therefore did not allow the jury to weigh the importance of the evidence themselves (O'Brian 2003). Indeed, one expert went as far as to say that 'he was sure that these ear prints were made by this defendant'.[47]

The Court of Appeal allowed the appeal not on the fact that the evidence was inadmissible but due to the fact that no forensic experts were put forward by the defence who refuted the reliability of this evidence type; the jury were disadvantaged. The Appeal Court said that 'Even so it seems to us that the fresh evidence, if not given at the trial, might reasonably have affected the approach of the crucial identification evidence of the experts and thus have affected the decision of the jury to convict'.[48]

While ear prints were a new science when introduced in *R v Dallagher*, this case and its appeal highlighted the ongoing issue that had plagued expert evidence, which is that of the reliability of expert evidence (The Law Commission 2011; Cunliffe 2013; Edmond et al. 2013; Edwards 2009; Roach 2009; Saks and Faigman 2008; Saks and Koehler 2008). Ear print evidence lacked a body of scientific research to underpin the conclusions that had been made by both of the experts in this case. There were no large databases or research which would support the creation of statistical analyses which could be applied to the analysis of the ear prints. In reality, multiple ear prints were taken from the suspect at different pressures and angles, which raises the suspicion that the prints being taken in such a manner was effectively a way to make these prints resemble those taken from the scene (Halpin 2008). The lack of scientific underpinning for this evidence type has been reflected in the increased realisation of the lack of reliability that is inherent not just in 'new' or 'novel' sciences such as this one but also in those sciences which have been utilised and presented in court and continue to be used and presented in court on multiple occasions, a fact that has been placed before the forensic science community with some force as a result of the recent reports into forensic science (The Law Commission 2011; National Research Council 2009; President's Council of Advisors on Science and Technology 2016).

In conclusion, a review of these high-profile miscarriages of justice have a number of common threads that run through them. Issues around the disclosure failings are common and unfortunately can still be found in the news reports.[49] Other failures, such as bias and reliability of evidence types, have attracted an increasing amount of research and investigation as a result of ongoing pressure on the sector, giving the forensic expert community the chance to address issues associated with these miscarriages of justice.

Notes

1. The Birmingham Six were convicted in 1975 of killing people in pub explosions in 1974. They had their convictions quashed in 1991.
2. *R v Sally Clarke* (2003) EWCA Crim 1020.
3. *R v Cannings* (2004) EWCA Crim 1.
4. https://www.innocenceproject.org/ (accessed 2018).
5. See *Davie v Edinburgh Magistrates* (1953) SC 34.
6. See http://www.telegraph.co.uk/news/nhs/12200115/Doctor-Waney-Squier-who-misled-courts-over-shaken-baby-syndrome-is-struck-off.html.
7. See https://www.theguardian.com/society/2016/nov/04/doctor-waney-squier-wins-appeal-shaken-baby-syndrome-trials-evidence.
8. See Disclosure: Expert's Evidence and Unused Material, https://www.cps.gov.uk/legal-guidance/disclosure-experts-evidence-case-management-and-unused-material-may-2010-guidance.
9. See Criminal Procedure Rules 2015, www.justice.gov.uk/criminal/procrules_fin/rulesmenu.htm.
10. See *R v Richard McIlkenny, Patrick Hill, William Power, John Walker, Robert Gerard Hunter and Hugh Callaghan* (1991) 93 Crim. App. R. 287.
11. See *R v Maguire Maguire, Smyth, Maguire, Maguire, O'Neill and Conlon* (1991) 94 Crim. App. R. 133.
12. See *R v Ward* (1993) 96 Crim. App. R. 1 at 52.
13. See *R v Richard McIlkenny, Patrick Hill, William Power, John Walker, Robert Gerard Hunter and Hugh Callaghan* (1991) 93 Crim. App. R. 287.
14. Ibid.
15. Ibid.
16. See *R v Maguire Maguire, Smyth, Maguire, Maguire, O'Neill and Conlon* (1991) 94 Crim. App. R. 133.
17. See *R v Ward* (1993) 96 Crim. App. R. 1 at 52.
18. Ibid.
19. See https://ccrc.gov.uk/about-us/.
20. *R v Clark* (2003) EWCA Crim 1020, (2003) All ER (D) 223 (Apr).
21. Ibid.
22. Ibid.
23. See Royal College of Pathologists, Sudden Unexpected Death in Infancy and Childhood, https://www.rcpath.org/discover-pathology/news/new-guidelines-for-the-investigation-of-sudden-unexpected-death-in-infancy-launched.html.

24. See CPS, Disclosure: Expert's Evidence and Unused Material, https://www.cps.gov.uk/legal-guidance/disclosure-experts-evidence-case-management-and-unused-material-may-2010-guidance.
25. See http://www.legislation.gov.uk/ukpga/1996/25/contents.
26. See CPS, Disclosure: Expert's Evidence and Unused Material, https://www.cps.gov.uk/legal-guidance/disclosure-experts-evidence-case-management-and-unused-material-may-2010-guidance.
27. See *Regina v H* (Appellant) (2003) (On Appeal from the Court of Appeal (Criminal Division)) *Regina v C* (Appellant) (On Appeal from the Court of Appeal (Criminal Division)) (Conjoined Appeals) available from https://publications.parliament.uk/pa/ld200304/ldjudgmt/jd040205/hc-1.htm.
28. *R v Adams* (2007) EWCA Crim 1, (2007) All ER (D) 25 (Jan).
29. *See R v Ward* (1993) 96 Crim. App. R. 1 at 52.
30. Ibid.
31. See Forensic Science Providers: Codes of Practice and Conduct, 2017, https://www.gov.uk/government/publications/forensic-science-providers-codes-of-practice-and-conduct-2017.
32. See Cognitive Bias Effects Relevant to Forensic Science Examinations, https://www.gov.uk/government/publications/cognitive-bias-effects-relevant-to-forensic-science-examinations.
33. See Control and Avoidance of Contamination in Crime Scene Examination Involving DNA Evidence Recovery, https://www.gov.uk/government/publications/crime-scene-dna-anti-contamination-guidance.
34. See Forensic Science Providers: Validation, https://www.gov.uk/government/publications/crime-scene-dna-anti-contamination-guidance.
35. See Code of Practice for Forensic Anthropology, https://www.gov.uk/government/consultations/code-of-practice-for-forensic-anthropology.
36. See The Fingerprint Inquiry Report, https://www.aridgetoofar.com/documents/TheFingerprintInquiryReport_Low_res.pdf.
37. *HM Advocate v McKie* (1999).
38. See The Fingerprint Inquiry Report, https://www.aridgetoofar.com/documents/TheFingerprintInquiryReport_Low_res.pdf.
39. *R v T* (2010) All ER (D) 240 (Oct); (2010) EWCA Crim 2439.
40. Ibid.
41. Ibid.
42. *R v Dennis Adams* (1996) 2 Crim. App. R. 467; *R v Adams* (No. 2) (1998) 1 Crim. App. R. 377; *R v Doheny* (1997) 1 Crim. App. R. 369.
43. *R v T* (2010) All ER (D) 240 (Oct); (2010) EWCA Crim 2439.
44. *Davie v Edinburgh Magistrates* (1953) SC 34.
45. Criminal Procedure Rules 2015 r. 19, http://www.justice.gov.uk/courts/procedure-rules/criminal/rulesmenu-2015#Anchor2.
46. See *R v Mark Dallagher* (2002) EWCA Crim 1903.
47. Ibid.
48. Ibid.
49. See https://www.theguardian.com/law/2018/jun/05/scores-of-uk-sexual-offence-cases-stopped-over-evidence-failings.

References

Budowle, B., Bottrell, M. C., Bunch, S. G., Fram, R., Harrison, D., Meagher, S., Oien, C. T., Peterson, P. E., Seiger, D. P. & Smith, M. B. 2009. A perspective on errors, bias, and interpretation in the forensic sciences and direction for continuing advancement. *Journal of Forensic Sciences*, 54, 798–809.

Champod, C., Evett, I. W. & Kuchler, B. 2001. Earmarks as evidence: A critical review. *Journal of Forensic Science*, 46, 1275–1284.

Cooley, C. M. & Turvey, B. E. 2014. Miscarriages of justice: Prevention and management. In: *Miscarriages of Justice: Actual Innocence, Forensic Evidence, and the Law*, p. 359.

Cunliffe, E. 2013. Independence, reliability and expert testimony in criminal trials. *Australian Journal of Forensic Sciences*, 45, 284–295.

Dror, I. E. & Hampikian, G. 2011. Subjectivity and bias in forensic DNA mixture interpretation. *Science & Justice*, 51, 204–208.

Edmond, G., Cole, S., Cunliffe, E. & Roberts, A. 2013. Admissibility compared: The reception of incriminating expert evidence (ie, forensic science) in four adversarial jurisdictions. *University of Denver Criminal Law Review*, 3, 31.

Edwards, H. T. 2009. Solving the problems that plague the forensic science community. *Jurimetrics*, 50, 5.

Garrett, B. L. & Neufeld, P. J. 2009. Invalid forensic science testimony and wrongful convictions. *Virginia Law Review*, 95, 1–97.

Gies, L. 2016. Miscarriages of justice in the age of social media: The Amanda Knox and Raffaele Sollecito innocence campaign. *British Journal of Criminology*, 57, 723–740.

Golan, T. 1999. The history of scientific expert testimony in the English courtroom. *Science in Context*, 12, 7–32.

Halpin, S. 2008. What have we got ear then: Developments in forensic science: Earprints as identification evidence at criminal trials. *UC Dublin Law Review*, 8, 65.

Hamer, D. 2012. Discussion paper: The *R v T* controversy: Forensic evidence, law and logic. *Law, Probability and Risk*, 11, 331–345.

Langdon, J. & Wilson, P. 2005. When justice fails: A follow-up examination of serious criminal cases since 1985. *Current Issues in Criminal Justice*, 17, 179.

The Law Commission. 2011. *Expert Evidence in Criminal Proceedings in England and Wales*. London: The Law Commission (Law Com No. 325).

Mason, J. 1986. Expert evidence in the adversarial system of criminal justice. *Medicine, Science and the Law*, 26, 8–12.

May, J. 1994. *Report of the Inquiry into the Circumstances Surrounding the Convictions Arising out of the Bomb Attacks in Guildford and Woolwich in 1974*, Final Report. *HC*, 449, 1993–1994.

Medwed, D. S. 2002. Actual innocents: Considerations in selecting cases for a new innocence project. *Nebraska Law Review*, 81, 1097.

Miller, L. S. 1984. Bias among forensic document examiners: A need for procedural change. *Journal of Police Science & Administration*, 12, 407–411.

Miller, L. S. 1987. Procedural bias in forensic science examinations of human hair. *Law and Human Behavior*, 11, 157–163.

Mnookin, J. L. 2007. Idealizing science and demonizing experts: An intellectual history of expert evidence. *Villanova Law Review*, 52, 763.

Morris, C. 2008. Court of Appeal—ear-print evidence. *Journal of Criminal Law*, 72, 488.
Mullin, C. 1997. *Error of Judgement: The Truth about the Birmingham Bombings*. Dublin, Ireland: Poolbeg Press.
National Research Council. 2009. *Strengthening Forensic Science in the United States: A Path Forward*. Washington, DC: National Academies Press.
Naughton, M. 2003. How big is the 'iceberg'? A zemiological approach to quantifying miscarriages of justice. *Radical Statistics*, 81, 5–17.
Naughton, M. 2004. Redefining miscarriages of justice: A revived human-rights approach to unearth subjugated discourses of wrongful criminal conviction. *British Journal of Criminology*, 45, 165–182.
Naughton, M. 2007. The official miscarriage of justice iceberg. In: *Rethinking Miscarriages of Justice*. Berlin: Springer, pp 37–52.
Nobles, R. & Schiff, D. 1995. Miscarriages of justice: A systems approach. *The Modern Law Review*, 58, 299–320.
Nobles, R. & Schiff, D. 2000. *Understanding Miscarriages of Justice: Law, the Media, and the Inevitability of Crisis*. Oxford University Press.
O'Brian Jr, W. E. 2003. Court scrutiny of expert evidence: Recent decisions highlight the tensions. *The International Journal of Evidence & Proof*, 7, 172–184.
Office of the Inspector General. 2006. *Review of the FBI's Handling of the Brandon Mayfield Case*. Washington, DC: Office of the Inspector General, Oversight and Review Division, U.S. Department of Justice.
President's Council of Advisors on Science and Technology. 2016. *Report to the President, Forensic Science in Criminal Courts: Ensuring Scientific Validity of Feature-Comparison Methods*. Washington, DC: Executive Office of the President of the United States, President's Council of Advisors on Science and Technology.
Redmayne, M. 1996. Expert evidence and scientific disagreement. *UC Davis Law Review*, 30, 1027.
Redmayne, M., Roberts, P., Aitken, C. & Jackson, G. 2011. Forensic science evidence in question. *Criminal Law Review*, 5, 347–356.
Rix, K. J. 1999. Expert evidence and the courts: 1. The history of expert evidence. *Advances in Psychiatric Treatment*, 5, 71–77.
Roach, K. 2009. Forensic science and miscarriages of justice: Some lessons from comparative experience. *Jurimetrics*, 67–92.
Runciman, W. G. & May, S. J. D. 1993. *The Royal Commission on Criminal Justice: Report*. London: HM Stationery Office.
Saks, M. J. & Faigman, D. L. 2008. Failed forensics: How forensic science lost its way and how it might yet find it. *Annual Review of Law and Social Science*, 4, 149–171.
Saks, M. J. & Koehler, J. J. 2008. The individualization fallacy in forensic science evidence. *Vanderbilt Law Review*, 61, 199.
Sangha, B., Moles, R. N. & Roach, K. 2010. *Forensic Investigations and Miscarriages of Justice: The Rhetoric Meets the Reality*. Toronto, ON: Irwin Law.
Savage, S. P., Grieve, J. & Poyser, S. 2007. Putting wrongs to right: Campaigns against miscarriages of justice. *Criminology & Criminal Justice*, 7, 83–105.
Schurr, B. 1993. *Expert Witnesses and the Duties of Disclosure & Impartiality: The Lessons of the IRA Cases in England*. Consultable ICI: http://www.aic.gov.au.

Tuerkheimer, D. 2009. The next innocence project: Shaken baby syndrome and the criminal courts. *Washington University Law Review*, 87, 1.

Vidmar, N. & Diamond, S. S. 2000. Juries and expert evidence. *Brooklyn Law Review*, 66, 1121.

Walker, C. 1999. Miscarriages of justice in principle and practice. In: Walker, C. & Starmer, K. (eds.) *Miscarriages of Justice. A Review of Justice in Error.* London: Blackstone, pp. 31–62.

Walker, C. & McCartney, C. 2008. Criminal justice and miscarriages of justice in England and Wales. In: Huff, C. R. & Killias, M. (eds.) *Wrongful Conviction.* Philadelphia, PA: Temple University Press, pp. 183–212.

Walker, C. & Stockdale, R. 1995. Forensic evidence and terrorist trials in the United Kingdom. *The Cambridge Law Journal*, 54, 69–99.

Ward, T. 2015. 'A new and more rigorous approach' to expert evidence in England and Wales? *The International Journal of Evidence & Proof*, 19, 228–245.

Warden, R. 2001. The revolutionary role of journalism in identifying and rectifying wrongful convictions. *UMKC Law Review*, 70, 803.

Expert Evidence in Scotland in Criminal Trials

A Defence Solicitor's Perspective

4

EAMON P. H. KEANE

Contents

4.1 Introduction

This chapter examines the practical issues surrounding the use and challenge of expert evidence from the perspective of the defence in criminal proceedings in Scotland.[1] It begins in Section 4.2 with a brief description of the Scottish legal system, alongside an introduction to the investigation and prosecution of crime in the jurisdiction, in order to provide context to the consideration of the specific legal and practical issues concerning the leading of expert evidence which follow thereafter in later sections. In Section 4.3 the applicable legal rules governing the leading of expert evidence in Scotland are considered briefly. Finally, Section 4.4 contains some of the author's personal experience of the use of expert evidence garnered from Scottish criminal trials that he has acted in and his reflections on the same, which it is hoped will enable readers to appreciate the practical reality of the topic.

4.2 The Scottish Legal System and the Investigation and Prosecution of Crime

4.2.1 The Scottish Legal System and Scottish Criminal Law

Scots law has a fascinating and rich history, marked notably by its assiduously guarded independence and its diverse sources.[2] The Scottish legal system is properly characterised as a hybrid legal system, containing elements of both the common and civilian legal traditions.[3] Today, Scots law is principally a common law jurisdiction, similar to the other legal jurisdictions which make up the United Kingdom, albeit it continues to be tempered by its historic roots in the civilian legal tradition which derive from when Scotland was itself an independent country. The sources of the Scots criminal law are generally speaking legislation, the common law and the 'institutional' writers.[4] Whereas there has been an understandable convergence with English law in many areas of Scots law over the years as a result of the union of the Crowns and Parliaments between Scotland and England, Scots criminal law has remained, to a large extent, resolutely distinct and independent in its nature.[5] Accordingly, the highest court of criminal *appeal* in Scotland is the High Court of Justiciary, which sits in Edinburgh, and subject to a small number of exceptions, every interlocutor and sentence pronounced by the High Court of Justiciary in Scots criminal matters is final.[6]

4.2.2 An Overview of the Structure of the Scottish Legal System

Scotland is divided into six Sheriffdoms on a geographical basis.[7] Each Sheriffdom is comprised of one or more areas known as 'sheriff court districts'.[8] Within each sheriff court district, a place is designated at which the judiciary of the Sheriffdom, known as 'sheriffs', are to sit and hold court for the purpose of exercising their judicial functions; these sittings are known as 'sheriff courts'.[9] In total presently there are thirty-nine sheriff courts in Scotland. The judge that presides in a sheriff court is called a Sheriff and she or he must be a qualified solicitor or advocate with at least 10 years' experience.[10]

There has also recently been created the office of 'summary sheriff'.[11] There are also a number of justice of the peace courts in Scotland located in sheriff court districts.[12] These courts are presided over by justices of the peace that do not have to be legally qualified.[13] There are two types of criminal procedure in Scotland, known as 'summary' and 'solemn' procedure, which will be considered in more detail later in the chapter. The type of procedure utilised is decided upon by the prosecutor, who takes a view on the appropriate choice of procedure dependent on the severity of the alleged offence and the associated sentence that can be imposed following conviction.[14] Summary procedure is used for less serious criminal offences and may occur in the sheriff, or justice of the peace court. Solemn procedure is used for more serious criminal offences. The majority of criminal prosecutions in Scotland occur in the sheriff court under summary procedure.[15] All sheriff and justice of the peace courts in Scotland are courts of first instance. As a *general* rule, the location of the alleged offence determines in which Sheriffdom the matter will be tried.[16] As mentioned previously, the High Court of Justiciary is the highest court of criminal appeal in Scotland.[17] The High Court of Justiciary has jurisdiction over the whole of Scotland and also sits as a court of first instance in Edinburgh, Glasgow and Aberdeen and occasionally in other Sheriffdoms as so required to deal with the most serious criminal offences.[18] Murder, rape and treason must always be prosecuted in the High Court.[19] Judges in the High Court of Justiciary are known as Lords Commissioner of Justiciary while presiding in that court.[20] These judges form the top tier of the judiciary in Scotland and also sit in the superior civil court in Scotland, the Court of Session.[21] They are selected from the ranks of advocates and solicitor advocates with five years' standing or full-time sheriffs who have held office for a period of 5 years.[22] The Lord Justice General is the head of the High Court of Justiciary.[23]

4.2.3 The Investigation and Prosecution of Criminal Offences in Scotland

The head of the criminal prosecution system in Scotland is the Lord Advocate.[24] In Scotland, the investigation of crime is carried out by the police acting under the general supervision of the Procurator Fiscal service and Crown Office. In practice, police in Scotland (and some other specialist reporting agencies) generally investigate potentially criminal matters of their own volition. [25] The public prosecution of criminal offences thereafter is the responsibility of the Lord Advocate and the Crown Office and Procurator Fiscal Service. Prosecutorial authorities in Scotland retain discretion as to whether they initiate criminal proceedings or not.[26] Some other public authorities can also initiate prosecution of individuals in respect of certain statutory offences; for example, educational authorities may prosecute parents in respect of the non-attendance at school of their children.[27] There is also a historical and rarely utilised system of private prosecution in Scotland.[28]

As mentioned previously, there are two types of criminal procedure in Scotland known as summary and solemn procedure which are utilised by the Crown depending generally on the severity of the alleged criminal offence.[29] The crucial difference between summary and solemn procedure relates to the trier of fact and the potential severity of disposal. Under summary procedure, the trier of fact is a judge (namely a justice of the peace, summary sheriff or sheriff) while under solemn procedure the trier of fact is a jury of 15 members of the public. Under solemn procedure a judge still presides over Scottish criminal trials to deal with matters of law that arise during the evidence and will charge the jury at the conclusion of all the evidence and the Crown and defence speeches on the legal rules they must follow when they retire to consider their verdict.

The archetypal case in summary procedure is initiated at the instance of the Procurator Fiscal by the signing of a document called a complaint which contains the charges which an accused person faces.[30] The Procurator Fiscal may crave a warrant for the apprehension and search of the accused, which will thereafter be passed to the police for execution, prior to serving the complaint.[31] Alternatively the complaint will simply be served on the accused with a citation to attend court on a particular date. The complaint is then 'called' at court and a plea tendered accordingly. The accused's status on bail will also be decided by the court at this point. If a not guilty plea is tendered, an intermediate and trial diet is assigned accordingly, albeit in some instances the requirement for an intermediate diet prior to trial is dispensed with. Summary procedure entails trial by a judge alone, who decides matters of fact and law and may return a verdict of 'guilty', 'not guilty' or 'not proven'.[32]

Solemn procedure in Scotland entails trial by a jury of 15 members of the public in either the sheriff court or the High Court of Justiciary and is utilised to deal with more serious crimes. In the archetypal case the local Procurator Fiscal will sign a document known as a petition which contains the charges against the accused, seeks warrant for his or her arrest and seeks the authority of the court to carry out certain other investigatory steps into the alleged crime. This document is presented to a sheriff who will sign it if it is *prima facie* competent and it is then passed to the police to execute accordingly.[33] The accused or 'the panel' will appear at the sheriff court after arrest (or of his or her own volition at the 'invite' of the Procurator Fiscal if it is decided not to pass the warrant to the police for execution) where the question of bail will be determined and the accused formally makes no plea in respect of the charges. If bail is granted then the accused is released and committed for further examination but no further court date is specified. If bail is refused then the accused will appear in eight day times for a diet of full committal where again no plea is tendered and the question of bail is further considered.[34] There are strict statutory deadlines regulating the progression of the case where an accused is remanded in custody or at liberty. The Crown carries out further preparation and investigation of its case and must disclose relevant evidence to the defence as matters progress.[35] The Crown will decide what charges (if any) the accused should ultimately face and a document will be drafted in the name of the Lord Advocate specifying these charges which is known as an indictment. The indictment also specifies the dates of further preparatory diets in the case (known as a 'first diet' if the matter is being prosecuted in the sheriff court or a 'preliminary hearing' if being tried in the High Court of Justiciary. Should the accused wish to plead guilty prior to the service of an indictment, then an accelerated procedure can be utilised under s.76 of the Criminal Procedure (Scotland) Act 1995. If the accused pleads not guilty, then the matter will proceed to trial where a jury of 15 members of the public determines matters of fact and the guilt or innocence of the accused while a presiding judge decides matters of law. The jury returns a verdict of either 'guilty', 'not guilty' or 'not proven' by a simple majority in contradistinction with the other legal systems of the United Kingdom, where only the verdicts of 'guilty' or 'not guilty' may be returned by a jury, usually composed of 12 members of the public, by way of unanimous verdict. Under both types of procedure the accused may be admitted to bail by the judge or remanded in custody to await trial accordingly.[36]

4.2.4 The Adversarial System of Proof

Scotland, along with the other two legal jurisdictions of the United Kingdom, England and Wales and Northern Ireland, employs an adversarial system of proof in contrast to the majority of the continental European judicial systems, which favour an inquisitorial approach.[37] Lord Justice Clerk Thomson described the adversarial systems as 'in essence a trial of skill between opposing parties, conducted under recognised rules and the prize is the judge's decision'.[38]

In Scotland, in the criminal context, the parties to the trial are the Crown and the defence, and they decide upon the issues to bring into play while the judge acts as a referee with the 'prize' being the verdict of the judge (or jury) depending on the procedure used. The trial proceeds largely on oral evidence produced by witnesses for either side.[39] The presumption of innocence, a fundamental principle of the Scottish judicial system, means that the Crown always carry the persuasive burden of proving the guilt of the accused beyond a reasonable doubt by the leading of corroborated evidence.[40] The judge operates to ensure that all the appropriate rules of evidence are followed and proceedings are accordingly fair. Regardless of whether solemn or summary procedure is used, the judge in modern Scots criminal procedure determines matters of law pertaining to the law of evidence, such as the relevancy of questioning and the admissibility of evidence. Questions of credibility, reliability and the 'weight' to be attached to the evidence of witnesses are reserved for the trier of fact. This will be the judge or jury as the case may be depending on whether the case is proceeding under summary or solemn procedure as explained earlier.

4.3 The Law Governing Expert Evidence in Scotland

4.3.1 Ordinary Witness and Opinion Evidence: Limitations Generally

As the purpose of the adversarial system is to seek to establish the *facts* of what may or may not have occurred, a witness called to give evidence is generally precluded from offering their *opinion* on the issue to be decided by the trier of fact and must confine their evidence to matters of fact within their own knowledge accordingly.[41] For example, during a robbery and assault trial, a question put by the defence to a Crown witness as to their opinion of whether the accused was actively involved in the robbery and assault was ruled as inadmissible as this was properly a matter for the jury as the trier of fact in the trial, not the witness, to determine.[42] However, it is important to bear in mind that witnesses in Scottish criminal trials do regularly give evidence which purports to be their opinion generally and this is in most cases admissible.[43] For example, a witness would be entitled to offer their understanding of what video footage seemed to show in a rape case where it is alleged that the complainer is unconscious during intercourse even though that issue is critical to the one that the jury has to decide.[44] Appropriate directions would be issued by a judge in such a case so as to emphasise to the jury that it is for them to decide what the footage does or does not show. Witnesses are also regularly asked during trials to describe the individual they believe they saw committing an offence. To some extent the distinction between fact and opinion evidence is therefore somewhat artificial and has been criticised as problematic.[45] If the witness's opinion evidence depends upon specialised expertise then that evidence will only be admissible if that individual is an established expert. The criteria for determining whether an individual is entitled to give expert evidence will be considered later in the chapter.

4.3.2 Expert Evidence – The Role of the Expert Witness

The role of the expert witness differs significantly from that of the ordinary witness. In Scotland, an expert or 'skilled witness' may be called to give opinion evidence if such evidence pertains to 'relevant matters which are not within the knowledge of everyday life reasonably to be imputed to a jury or other finder of fact', and such evidence is admissible 'if it is likely to assist the jury or finder of fact in the proper determination of the issue before it'.[46] In essence, therefore the role of the expert witness is to offer opinion evidence to *assist* the trier of fact to assess and understand other evidence presented, in its specialist and often scientific context, and to further allow the trier of fact to properly understand the impact of that evidence upon the *matter in issue* before them. The expert witness cannot therefore give opinion evidence on matters that are within the knowledge and experience of the trier of fact or give evidence that merely serves to bolster or undermine a witness's credibility.[47] It is crucial that the evidence of the expert witness must also be relevant to the matter at issue and not related to collateral issues, be based on a recognised and developed academic discipline and follow a developed methodology.[48] Further, the opinion evidence must produce a result which is capable of being assessed and given more or less weight in light of all the evidence before the finder of fact.[49] The evidence upon which the expert's opinion is based still requires to be established.[50] The expert witness cannot be asked to express an opinion on whether a crucial fact has been established 'beyond reasonable doubt' as this is a matter for the jury.[51] As such in a culpable homicide case, where the deceased was suffering from heart disease and there were other stressful factors present, such as the consumption of alcohol and physical exertion, it was held to be improper to ask a doctor whether he could be satisfied 'beyond reasonable doubt' that an attack by the accused had caused the deceased's death. The expert witness should instead have been asked how confident they were of the opinions which they expressed or whether they regarded the issue as difficult or doubtful.[52]

Finally, in Scotland, there is no obligation on the trial judge to summarise all the evidence for the jury at the conclusion of the trial regardless of whether there has been conflicting expert opinion or not as the judge's principal duty is merely to direct upon the applicable law.[53] It is a matter for the Crown and defence as to how to present their cases. Beyond the requirement for the trial judge to direct on the law, it has been said that all that is required is such direction so as to allow a hypothetical informed observer to understand the verdict that is eventually reached by the jury.[54] However, in murder and culpable homicide cases where there is a realistic possibility of an unknown case of death and complex and scientific expert evidence has been led, it *is* incumbent on the trial judge to direct the jury that they must exclude this possibility before they can convict and to give the jury guidance by way of a succinct, balanced review of the central factual matters for their determination, including conflicting medical expert opinion.[55] The failure to do so has been held to result in a miscarriage of justice due to a material misdirection by omission, and convictions have been quashed by the High Court of Justiciary on appeal accordingly.[56]

4.3.3 Expert Witnesses – Establishing Expertise

Not everyone is entitled to give expert evidence. The credentials of an expert witness (namely their experience, qualifications and expertise) should be established by the party calling that witness before any evidence is led. This usually occurs, without dispute, simply by asking the witness to speak to their relevant qualifications and experience, which will usually be detailed in the expert report they have prepared (which will be lodged as a production at the court). The judge has an overarching duty to exclude evidence if he or she deems that the credentials of the expert witness to give opinion evidence have not been established.[57] This duty operates regardless of whether a challenge is made by either the prosecution or the defence to the credentials of the expert.[58] Unlike in other jurisdictions, there is no set procedure in Scotland whereby the admissibility of expert witness testimony can be determined by the judge acting as a 'gatekeeper' at a hearing prior to trial.[59]

4.3.4 Expert Obligations to the Court

An expert witness used by either the Crown or defence has an obligation to the court if a report of theirs has been lodged as a production regardless of whether they are ultimately cited to give evidence or not by either party. The expert needs to appreciate that regardless of who they are instructed by, there is an overriding obligation upon them to give independent, objective, unbiased opinion evidence only on matters within their expertise. The expert witness must also be clear that their opinion evidence is provisional if insufficient data is available to reach any conclusion and must be candid about stating any qualifications relating to the accuracy of their conclusions.[60] Unlike in England and Wales, experts still enjoy immunity from suit in Scotland in relation to the evidence they give and reports they produce during proceedings.[61]

4.3.5 Further Practical Considerations

Finally, what follows is a basic explanation of the practical mechanics of the leading of expert evidence in criminal trials in Scotland. As mentioned previously, the adversarial system still favours oral evidence as a singular feature of proof.[62] Therefore unless an expert's evidence can be agreed by way of joint minute the expert will be required to attend court and give oral evidence. Due to the requirements of the corroboration rule in Scotland, if the instructed expert's opinion evidence relates to the essential facts of the Crown case (i.e., the commission of the crime or identification of the accused) then it will require to be corroborated.[63] In practice, if certain basic issues are not in dispute, such as the classification of illegal drugs, then the terms of the Crown's forensic report will simply be agreed prior to trial. There is limited provision for certain matters to be taken as proven without the attendance of experts in certain types of cases.[64]

During criminal proceedings, if an expert report prepared by either the Crown or the defence is signed by two authorised scientists and is duly intimated, then unless a challenge is made in terms of the act, the report will be held to sufficient evidence of the qualifications, facts and conclusions reached therein.[65] However, these facts and conclusions can of course still be attacked as to their credibility and reliability in cross-examination. The statutory duty of disclosure incumbent upon the Crown means that expert reports must always be disclosed to the defence in advance of trial.[66] There is no corresponding obligation upon the defence to disclose any expert reports complied on behalf of the accused. Under solemn procedure, however, there is a general obligation to notify the Crown of the defence that is being followed.[67] Further, should the defence wish to call an expert witness to give evidence, then the expert's report will be lodged *in causa* as a production which will allow the Crown to consider it and instruct their own expert witness should they so wish.[68] The Crown also retains the right to precognosce the defence expert prior to trial should they be listed as a defence witness. An expert called to give evidence for either side is liable to cross-examination in the same manner as any witness and regularly has the validity of their opinions challenged and attacks made on the accuracy of the methodology used.

4.4 Expert Evidence: Personal Reflections

The final section of this chapter reflects upon the author's personal experience of the use of expert evidence in Scottish criminal trials from his time in private practice. The opinions offered are accordingly the author's own. Names of cases have been made alphabetised so as to preserve anonymity.[69]

4.4.1 Access to Experts: Funding

The first practical matter that needs to be considered is access to expert opinion generally. In this context, a crucial and often insurmountable issue is that of funding. In cases where the accused is funding his representation privately, this is not usually an issue for the defence, albeit expert instruction fees can be expensive; however, where the accused is eligible for legal aid then issues can and do regularly arise in respect of funding. Any instruction of an expert to give evidence or provide a report for a legally aided individual must first be approved or 'sanctioned' by the Scottish Legal Aid Board (hereafter 'the board') before the instruction can proceed.[70] This process entails acquiring a quote from the expert the defence wishes to instruct and thereafter seeking sanction from the Scottish Legal Aid Board via an online application process. The defence is required to justify the cost of the expert by illustrating how the report of the expert will be of material assistance to the preparation of the accused's defence, or will materially undermine the case against them.[71] In some types of cases, such as those involving drugs, firearms or certain road traffic offences, the sanction of funding to instruct an expert is granted almost as a matter of course. This occurs ostensibly in tacit recognition of the importance of expert evidence in these sorts of cases where expert opinion is likely to be crucial to the accused's defence. In these cases 'templates' can be used online to progress the application and minimal information is sought from the board with set rates being offered.[72] If the instruction of an expert is sought out with these situations, known as the instruction of a 'non-templated' expert during the online application process, then the board is, in my experience, highly likely to refuse to grant sanction. This is especially so when the accused is being tried under summary procedure. The refusal of sanction from the board will state that part of the reason for such refusal is that the cost of instructing such an expert would be 'disproportionate' and not 'a reasonable use of public funds'.

Under solemn procedure, issues pertaining to access can also arise albeit usually in a different manner. Sanction is generally more readily available for the instruction of experts, and issues in relation to 'disproportionate' cost are less likely to arise in my experience. That being said, it is common to have sanction refused initially only to have it granted when multiple reconsideration requests have been submitted. This process often entails a negotiation of sorts between the solicitor and the prospective instructed expert as the board, in refusing sanction, will often state that the price quoted for the work by the expert is too high. The board also commonly asks for a detailed breakdown of the quote provided by the expert, including a specification of the anticipated time involved in preparatory work, travel and the actual writing of the report and other matters. The board will often also ask the solicitor to provide alternative quotes for the expert analysis considered if the quote provided exceeds a certain level of expenditure (approximately £800) or involves unusual work.[73]

Another issue that can arise in respect of funding occurs in cases where sanction for counsel has been granted, usually where a prosecution is occurring in the High Court of Justiciary.[74] A recurrent problem in these cases is the difficulty in getting the board to sanction counsel to attend consultations with experts (instructed on either the defence or Crown's behalf) prior to trial. In such a case, sanction has to be sought in advance for counsel to meet the expert as this work is not covered under the general grant of sanction for counsel's fees in the case.[75] In my experience, the board frequently seeks to refuse such applications on the basis that the instructing solicitor can simply precognosce the instructed expert themselves. While the logic of this position can be understood, in cases involving complex scientific opinion evidence the practical result can cause understandable concern to counsel who have to conduct the trial. Sanction is usually granted eventually if the defence repeatedly seeks to challenge the board's refusal, but the process itself is time-consuming and frustrating, especially so when there is a trial diet in close proximity. In my experience, Crown experts have generally made themselves readily available for such consultations should they be so required, and no practical issues have ever arisen in that regard. It is worth stating that in my experience, expert witnesses in Scotland tend to mindful of their overarching ethical obligations as outlined above.

4.4.2 Experts in Use: Case A

It is perhaps useful at this point to narrate a straightforward example of a case where expert evidence has had a practical effect on the outcome for the accused. Regularly, in summary and solemn criminal trials expert opinion evidence is led by the Crown and defence as to whether the quantity, value and circumstances surrounding the seizure of drugs indicate personal use or the more serious charge of possession with intent to supply.[76] Expert witnesses are often asked for their opinion on certain facts established (such as the quantity of drugs and the circumstances surrounding their seizure) so as to assist the trier of fact in properly deciding the issue before them, namely, whether the accused is guilty of simple possession or the more serious offence of possession with intent to supply. In the case of A, A was charged by way of summary complaint with possession with intent to supply diamorphine (also known as heroin), a class A drug which is an offence under Section 5(3) of the Misuse of Drugs Act 1971. A bag had been recovered on his person following a search by police under the auspices of the aforementioned Misuse of Drugs Act 1971 containing 9.2 grams of diamorphine. A's position was that he had recently bought the drugs in bulk for his own use, as he suffered from a serious drug addiction, and that he had no intention of supplying the drugs in question to others. A plea was canvassed with the Crown at the pleading diet to an amended charge libelling simple possession, but this was not accepted by the procurator fiscal depute in court. A subsequently pleaded not guilty to the charge and was remanded in custody, bail having been refused due to his record of previous convictions. A drug expert was instructed upon behalf of the defence to express an opinion on the quantity of the drugs and the circumstances surrounding their seizure. The report concluded that the weight and arrangement of the drugs was not in any known 'dealing' measure and that in the absence of any other facts suggesting that A was involved in supply (such as quantities of cash or the drug being held in individual bags known to be used in the process of sale) then, in the expert's opinion, the drugs may well have been for personal use. The report was intimated to the Crown, who thereafter decided to accept a plea to the lesser charge of of possession. A Community Payback Order incorporating supervision and unpaid work was subsequently imposed by the sheriff.[77] If A had pleaded guilty to the more serious offence of possession with intent to supply, it is almost inevitable that he would have received a significant custodial sentence from the court. The reader can hopefully discern from this example how the logistics of the instruction of expert witnesses play out within the Scottish criminal trial and the important practical effect that expert evidence can have on the eventual trial outcome.

4.4.3 Delay and Expert Reports: Case B

One commonly encountered issue in my own jurisdiction is the adjournment and in some instances desertion of proceedings which occurs due to the failure of the prosecution to produce timely expert opinion reports in cases concerning charges which allege contravention of the Misuse of Drugs Act 1971. In such instances, the prosecution will always require a forensic report containing expert opinion indicating the illicit substance in question, its quantity and its value, as such evidence will be crucial to proof of their case. In cases concerning more serious charges, such as being concerned in the supply of drugs, the prosecution will seek to produce an expert opinion report commenting on whether the facts and circumstances surrounding seizure are indicative of that more serious offence, as again this evidence will be essential, as outlined previously. The prosecution regularly seeks to adjourn trials on the basis that these reports simply haven't been completed in time. The excuse mainly offered for this delay is that the facility which undertakes this work is overworked (the inference drawn by the author that such facilities are also underfunded). On occasion, the Crown will also submit that administrative errors in their own office has led to a failure to progress matters. The defence may choose to oppose such a motion. Whether such a motion of adjournment is granted or not is a question for the presiding judge, who will require to consider whether the granting of such a motion is in the interests of justice taking into account the balancing of interests of the various parties involved, namely, prejudice to the prosecution, prejudice to the accused and prejudice to the public interest.[78] To illustrate the extent of the problem consider the case of B.[79] B was charged initially under solemn procedure with *inter alia* being concerned in the supply of cannabis and diazepam after quantities of both drugs were found at his property. The charges specified that B was concerned in the supply of the drugs on a date in January 2015. He appeared on petition under solemn procedure at the first calling of the case on 18 March 2015 and made no plea or declaration and was admitted to bail. The Crown subsequently decided to proceed by way of summary procedure and so a complaint was served on the accused under the procedure described earlier in the chapter. He subsequently tendered a not guilty plea to the charges on that complaint on 8 July 2015 at a pleading diet. At an intermediate diet on 10 September 2015 the Crown moved to adjourn the upcoming trial on 12 October 2015 as they indicated neither forensic nor statement of opinion expert reports were ready in respect of the drugs seized. As mentioned previously, these reports are considered essential in a prosecution of this type. The motion was unopposed by the defence. A new intermediate and trial diet was set for 27 October 2015 and 23 November 2015. At the intermediate diet the Crown again moved to adjourn the trial diet on the basis of the unavailability of the reports discussed above. The defence opposed the motion on this occasion submitting that, in the first instance, whatever the reason behind the delay of the reports, the Crown was at fault and further, given the amount of time that passed since the alleged offence, should the motion be granted, the prejudice to the accused outweighed the prejudice to the Crown and the public interest.[80] The sheriff agreed and refused the Crown's motion. The Crown sought a continued intermediate diet to allow further investigation to be made into the status of the reports. A continued intermediate diet was accordingly assigned for 19 November 2015 a few days prior to trial. At the continued intermediate diet the Crown again moved to adjourn the trial claiming again that logistical and administrative issues had caused the delay in the preparation of the expert drug reports. The defence renewed their opposition in the same terms as previously described. The sheriff again refused the Crown's motion. On 20 November 2015, 3 days prior to the trial diet, the Crown indicated to the defence that they would no longer be seeking a conviction against B, allowing the complaint to fall and bringing an end to the prosecution entirely.[81] In the author's opinion, the issue illustrated here should be viewed as symptomatic of the wider issue of the lack of proper funding at present in the criminal justice system in Scotland and the sometimes unjust results which can arise therefrom.

4.5 Conclusion

It is hoped that this chapter has allowed the reader to appreciate both the legal principles and practicalities surrounding the use of expert evidence in criminal trials in Scotland. As in any area of publicly funded legal work, funding remains an ever-present and often insurmountable issue. This factor often renders the potential use of expert evidence practically impossible by the defence. As has also been illustrated, the issue of underfunding can also lead to severe consequences for the Crown. Justice, ultimately, suffers due to these funding issues.

That being said, as will no doubt be evident from other chapters in this edition, the field of forensic science is rapidly developing, and with such rapid development comes a multitude of possibilities and, potentially, problems for the criminal justice system in Scotland. The pace of scientific development and the potential for greater use of digital information technology resonates throughout many current debates concerning the modernisation of the Scottish legal system. The current Lord Justice General has expressed repeatedly his willingness to see the radical reform of and modernisation in the arena of criminal procedure generally. It is interesting that one could argue, that the High Court of Justiciary on appeal appears to have adopted a somewhat conservative approach to the admissibility of expert evidence in recent years, especially in the field of developing areas of scientific practice. It will be interesting to see how matters progress over the coming years.[82] The topic of expert evidence in criminal trials is certainly an area that merits serious consideration in the ongoing reform of Scottish legal system in the opinion of the author. It is hoped that serious consideration will be given in the future to questions such as whether a statutory test governing admissibility on the grounds of reliability is desirable in Scotland and whether there perhaps should be greater judicial scientific training generally to assist in the determination of admissiblity. In the civil context, it is apparent that advances have been made in the field of expert evidence in Scotland.[83] It is hoped that a similarly innovative and proactive approach is taken in the criminal sphere in the future.

Notes

1. The author is a qualified solicitor in Scotland who practises predominantly in the field of criminal defence.
2. For a more comprehensive analysis see Andrew Dewar Gibb, *Law from over the Border: A Short Account of a Strange Jurisdiction* (Edinburgh, W. Green & Son, 1950).
3. For further detail see Gloag and Henderson, *The Law of Scotland* (Edinburgh, W. Green, 2012) 3–39.
4. The institutional writers are, broadly speaking, a series of jurists that produced works in the sixteenth, seventeenth and eighteenth centuries seeking to collate and posit the principles underpinning the Scottish legal system. For a fuller account see David M. Walker, *A Legal History of Scotland V: The Eighteenth Century* (Edinburgh, T. & T. Clark, 1998) 1–42.
5. It is interesting to note that following the Act of Union in 1707 between Scotland and England an appellate jurisdiction developed in the House of Lords (latterly the Supreme Court of the United Kingdom) for Scots civil appeals; however, no such jurisdiction arose in criminal matters. For further analysis see Alan Paterson, *Final Judgment: The Last Law Lords and the Supreme Court* (Oxford, Hart Publishing, 2013) 233–245.

6. As per the Criminal Procedure (Scotland) Act 1995 S.124(2). See also *Mackintosh v Lord Advocate* (1876) 3 R. (H.L.) 34. The limited exceptions to this principle relevant in the Scots criminal context are the jurisdiction of the Supreme Court of the United Kingdom to review 'compatibility issues'. A compatibility issue concerns whether a public authority in Scotland (which includes the Lord Advocate and courts) has acted or proposes to act in a way that is incompatible with the European Convention on Human Rights or EU law or whether an act of the Scottish Parliament is incompatible with any of the convention rights or EU law. See the Criminal Procedure (Scotland) Act 1995, S.288ZA(2) and the Supreme Court, 'The Jurisdiction of the Supreme Court of the United Kingdom in Scottish Appeals: Human Rights, the Scotland Act 2012 and the Courts Reform (Scotland) Act 2014', https://www.supremecourt.uk/docs/jurisdiction-of-the-supreme-court-in-scottish-appeals.pdf (accessed Feb 2, 2016).
7. These are Glasgow and Strathkelvin, Grampian, Highland and Islands, Lothian and Borders, North Strathclyde, South Strathclyde, Dumfries and Galloway and Tayside and Central and Fife. See S.1 of the Courts Reform (Scotland) Act 2014.
8. S.1(2) of the Courts Reform (Scotland) Act 2014.
9. S.1(3) of the Courts Reform (Scotland) Act 2014.
10. See S.4 of the Courts Reform (Scotland) Act 2014. Sheriffs are appointed by the queen on the recommendation of the First Minister on the recommendation of the Judicial Appointments Board for Scotland and in consultation with the Lord President of the Court of Session as per S.95 of the Scotland Act 1998 and S.11 of the Judiciary and Courts (Scotland) Act 2008.
11. As per S.5 of the Courts Reform (Scotland) Act 2014.
12. See S.59 Criminal Proceedings, etc. (Reform) (Scotland) Act 2007.
13. S.67 of the Criminal Proceedings, etc. (Reform) (Scotland) Act 2007. Justices of the peace are appointed in the name of her Majesty the Queen by the Scottish ministers.
14. Unless determined otherwise by legislation, under summary procedure in the justice of the peace court the maximum sentence is a fine not exceeding £2500 or a period of imprisonment not exceeding 60 days; under summary procedure in the sheriff court the maximum sentence is a fine not exceeding £10,000 or a period of imprisonment not exceeding 12 months; under solemn procedure in the sheriff court the maximum sentence is an unlimited fine or a period of imprisonment not exceeding 5 years; the sentencing powers of the High Court of Justiciary are unlimited. See S.5 and S.3(3) of the Criminal Procedure (Scotland) Act 1995.
15. Of the 82,716 convictions recorded in Scottish Courts in 2018–61% (50,635) occurred in the sheriff court under summary procedure, 33% (27,410) in justice of the peace courts, with High Court and sheriff solemn convictions accounting for only approximately 6% (5,316) cumulatively. See the Scottish Government, 'Criminal Proceedings in Scotland, 2018–, https://www.gov.scot/publications/criminal-proceedings-scotland-2017-18/(accessed Feb 21, 2019).
16. See Sir Gerald Gordon QC, *The Criminal Law of Scotland* (Edinburgh: W. Greene, 2000) 96–98.
17. It should be noted, however, that the recently established Sheriff Appeal Court now hears appeals from summary criminal procedures; see S.47 and S.118 of the Courts Reform (Scotland) Act 2014.

18. The High Court of Justiciary may try any offence that is 'indictable' in Scotland; see S.3(2) of the Criminal Procedure (Scotland) Act 1995.
19. See S.3(6) of the of the Criminal Procedure (Scotland) Act 1995.
20. S.1(2) of the Criminal Procedure (Scotland) Act 1995.
21. Ibid.
22. S.20A of the Judiciary and Courts (Scotland) Act 2008.
23. See S.1(1) of the Criminal Procedure (Scotland) Act 1995. Since 1836 the office of the Lord Justice General has been combined with that of the Lord President of the Court of Session, the head of the civil system of justice in Scotland, and the role has accordingly been fulfilled by the same individual since that time.
24. The Lord Advocate is a member of the Scottish Government. He or she is appointed by the Queen on the recommendation of the First Minister of the Scottish Government, who acts with the agreement of the Scottish Parliament in making such a recommendation. See the Scotland Act 1998 S.44(1)(c) and S.48(5)(c).
25. The police theoretically act upon the instruction of the procurator fiscal in investigating crime, albeit in practice this occurrence is rare and confined to more serious or complicated cases. See *Smith v Her Majesty's Advocate* (1952) J.C. at 71. The Crown Office and Procurator Fiscal Service also has responsibility for investigating sudden and suspicious deaths in Scotland and allegations of criminal conduct made against the police along with the assessment and possession of certain types of property.
26. Procurator fiscals are as a matter of law independent of the Lord Advocate; however, they are *de facto* under an obligation to obey his instructions and are as such commonly and correctly viewed as acting under his authority. Procurators fiscal are paid employees of the Crown who hold a commission from the Lord Advocate to prosecute in his name. From here on in, the term 'Crown' is used to refer to the Lord Advocate, the Procurator Fiscal Service and the prosecution generally, whil the term 'defence' is used to designate those acting for the accused.
27. See S.43(2) of the Education Scotland Act 1980.
28. Individuals seeking to bring private prosecutions require first to seek 'concurrence' from the Lord Advocate before seeking the grant of a criminal bill of letters from the High Court of Justiciary as per *Robertson v HM Advocate* (1892) 3 White 230. If the Lord Advocate refuses to grant concurrence to the private prosecution, the High Court of Justiciary may nevertheless grant the bill of letters authorising the private prosecution, although reported instances of such occurrences are extremely rare. See *X v Sweeney* (1982) J.C. 70 for one such example of a bill of letters being obtained.
29. And the likely sentence if the accused is convicted. In some instances, the common law or statue will dictate which procedure should be used. For a detailed exploration of the practicalities of each procedure see Renton and Brown, *Criminal Procedure* (Edinburgh, W. Greene, 2016) 1:08–1:16.
30. See S.138(1) of the Criminal Procedure Scotland Act 1995.
31. For a more detailed exploration of criminal procedure including the role of the police see Renton and Brown, *Criminal Procedure* (Edinburgh, W. Greene, 2016) 5:01–7:34.
32. Either a Sheriff, Summary Sheriff or Justice of the Peace depending on the alleged severity of the offence and forum chosen for prosecution by the Crown.

33. Even if the accused has been arrested without warrant, when he or she appears from custody a petition will still be presented to the sheriff to sign craving arrest and search.
34. It is competent for the Crown to proceed straight to the service of an indictment without having the accused appear on petition.
35. S.65 of the Criminal Procedure (Scotland) Act 1995.
36. See S.23C of the Criminal Procedure (Scotland) Act 1995 for the grounds relevant to the grant or refusal of bail.
37. For further see Eamon Keane and Fraser Davidson, *Raitt onEvidence: Principle, Policy and Practice* (Edinburgh, Greene & Son, 2018) 1–7.
38. *Thomson v Glasgow Corporation* (1961) S.L.T. 237 at 246.
39. For a criticism of this approach, specifically its reliance on the memory of witnesses, see Lord Carloway, 'Scots Criminal Evidence and Procedure – Meeting the Challenges and Expectations of Modern Society and Legal Thinking', http://www.scotland-judiciary.org.uk/Upload/Documents/CriminalLawConferenceMurrayfield9May2013.pdf (accessed Dec 10, 2015).
40. Unless statue dictates that corroboration is not required. By way of explanation, in Scots law currently the unique corroboration rule states that the crucial facts in a criminal trial, namely the identification of the accused and the commission of the offence, cannot be established by the evidence of one witness alone. A number of exceptions to the rule have developed over time. The abolition of corroboration was proposed following the Carloway Review; Report and Recommendations (Scottish Government, 2011) and has been hotly debated by the profession and public ever since. An expert review group was subsequently established to examine the safeguards that would be required to prevent miscarriages of justice if corroboration was abolished. The current Scottish government had proposed legislation to remove the requirement in the Criminal Justice (Scotland) Bill 2013, although the bill was delayed and the provisions concerning abolition were eventually removed before its enaction. It seems that for the immediate future, at least, the corroboration rule is here to stay.
41. *Fraser v HM Advocate* (2011) HCJAC 17.
42. *Kelso v HM Advocate* (1990) SCCR 9.
43. See Margaret Ross and James Chalmers, *Walker & Walker, the Law of Evidence in Scotland* (Edinburgh, Bloomsbury, 2015) 295–297.
44. *Ronald v HM Advocate* (2007) SCCR 466. It should be noted that once the provenance of such footage has been established, it becomes real evidence in the case and may be interpreted by the trier of fact alone, notwithstanding that no witnesses have spoken to their opinion of what it shows as per *Gubinas v HM Advocate* 2017 SCCR 463.
45. See Eamon Keane and Fraser Davidson, *Raitt on Evidence: Principle, Policy and Practice* (Edinburgh, Greene & Son, 2018) 51.
46. As per *Young v HM Advocate* 2014 S.L.T. 21.
47. *HMA v Grimmond* 2002 S.L.T. 508. It should be noted that in the wake of this case, specific statutory provisions were enacted which provided a significant if limited relaxation on the rules relating to the admissibility of expert evidence regarding credibility in sexual offences cases. See s.275(C) of the Criminal Procedure (Scotland) Act 1995 and the *obiter* comments of the High Court of Justiciary in *CJM v HMA* 2013 S.C.C.R 215.

48. As per Lord Menzies at para. 54 of *Young v HMA* (2014) S.L.T. 21. See also the Supreme Court's judgment in *Kennedy v Cordia Services LLP* (2016) UKSC 6 where it was noted that the trial judge has to determine whether the proposed skilled evidence will assist the court in its task, whether the witness has the necessary knowledge and experience, whether the witness is impartial in the presentation and assessment of the evidence, and whether there is a reliable body of knowledge and experience to underpin the expert's evidence. Although the case related to a Scots civil appeal it is still influential in the criminal context see *Jones v HMA*, (2016) HCJAC 65.
49. Ibid. *Young v HMA* (2014) S.L.T 21. and para, 49 of *Hainey v HMA* (2013) S.L.T. 525.
50. *Blogojevic v HMA*, 1995 S.L.T. 1189.
51. *Hendry v HMA* (1988) S.L.T. 25.
52. Ibid.
53. In contrast with the position in England and Wales see, for example, the Criminal Procedure Rules 2014 (si 2014/1610) r.38.14(2)(b)).
54. *Shahid Ramzan v HMA* (2015) HCJAC 9 at para. 34.
55. As per *Walker v HMA* (2011) S.L.T. 1114 and *Hainey v HMA* 2013 S.L.T. 525.
56. Ibid.
57. *Hainey v HMA* (2013) S.L.T. 525.
58. Ibid.
59. See, for example, the position in England and Wales under Rule 33.6 of the Criminal Procedure Rules.
60. See *National Justice Compania Naviera SA v Prudential Assurance Co Ltd* (1993) 2 Lloyd's Rep. 68 for further articulation in an English case of what those duties have been held to mean. See also *Hainey v HMA* (2013) S.L.T. 525.
61. See *Amy Whitehead's Legal Representative v Graeme John Douglas and Another* (2006) CSOH 178 and *Watson v McEwan* [1905] AC 480.
62. For a criticism of this approach see the comments of the then Lord Justice Clerk, now Lord Justice General Carloway in 'Scots Criminal Evidence and Procedure – Meeting the Challenges and Expectations of Modern Society and Legal Thinking', http://www.scotland-judiciary.org.uk/Upload/Documents/CriminalLawConferenceMurrayfield9May2013.pdf REPETITION.
63. S.256–S.258 of the Criminal Procedure Scotland Act 1995.
64. See S.280–S.284 of the Criminal Procedure Scotland Act 1995.
65. S. 280 of the Criminal Procedure Scotland Act 1995.
66. See S.121 Criminal Justice and Licensing (Scotland) Act 2010.
67. See the obligations imposed upon the defence under 70A of the Criminal Procedure Scotland Act 1995.
68. See also the procedure under S.280 as explained above.
69. All data is on file with the author.
70. Regulation 14(1) of the Criminal Legal Aid (Scotland) Regulations 1996.
71. See the Scottish Legal Aid Board Criminal Legal Assistance Handbook.
72. To give an example, generally around £300 is authorised for a report on the quantity and value of drugs.
73. See 16.83 of the Scottish Legal Aid Board Criminal Legal Assistance Handbook.
74. There is a split legal profession in Scotland made up of solicitors, solicitor-advocates and advocates. Only solicitor-advocates and advocates have rights of audience to appear in the superior courts such as the High Court of Justiciary. The term 'counsel' is used to refer to advocates.

75. Ibid. 16.20.
76. S.5(2) and S.5(3) of the Misuse of Drugs Act 1971, respectively.
77. Such an order is competent as an alternative to imprisonment in terms of s. 227A of the Criminal Procedure (Scotland) Act 1995.
78. *Tudhope v Lawrie* (1979) J.C. 44. *Patterson v Procurator Fiscal, Airdrie* (2012) HCJAC 61.
79. Data on file with author.
80. As per the relevant test set out in *Tudhope v Lawrie* (1979) J.C. 44.
81. The problem detailed here is not at all uncommon. See the reported case of *Bowden v PF Glasgow* (2015) HCJAC 11.
82. See *Hainey v HMA* (2013) S.L.T. 525 and *Young v HM Advocate* (2014) S.L.T. 21.
83. For example, in the judgement of the Inner House of the Court of Session in *SSE Generation Ltd v Hochtief Solutions Ltd AG* (2016), CSOH 117 Lord Woolman noted that a process known as 'hot-tubbing' of experts had been followed by parties. Such a process involves experts giving evidence simultaneously presided over by a judge. The experts may challenge each others' opinions and conclusions and parties may of course still cross-examine them too. Lord Woolman noted that he found the process 'extremely valuable'.

The Role of the Expert Witness in the Northern Ireland Criminal Justice System

5

JONATHAN DOAK AND TIM JEBB

Contents

5.1 Introduction

This chapter explores the role of the expert witness in Northern Ireland criminal proceedings. For the most part, the rules governing expert evidence in Northern Ireland mirror those of England and Wales. There are, however, a number of procedural differences, and the rules themselves are generally found in delegated legislation; the Criminal Procedure Rules do not apply to Northern Ireland. By the same token, decisions of the English Court of Appeal and the Supreme Court on matters pertaining to English law are not binding on the Northern Ireland courts, although they are typically followed in practice. As in the rest of the United Kingdom, there is no set definition of an expert witness, nor are there any specific qualifications he or she must have before being called to give evidence. The only exception relates to findings of unfitness to plead. In these circumstances, Article 49 of the Mental Health (Northern Ireland) Order 1986 provides that this question must be determined by the judge alone on the basis of the oral evidence of an appointed medical practitioner and on the written or oral evidence of one other medical practitioner.

In general terms, competency in a particular field will be a question for the judge to determine within a *voir dire*.[1] It will be for the party calling the witness to establish, on the balance of probabilities, that the witness is competent to give an expert opinion to the court. The English Court of Appeal has been unequivocal that all expert evidence must have a reliable scientific basis. In *R v Dlugosz and Others*,[2] it stated that it was 'essential to recall the principle which is applicable, namely in determining the issue of admissibility, the court must be satisfied that there is a sufficiently reliable scientific basis for the evidence to be admitted. If there is then the court leaves the opposing views to be tested before the jury'.[3] To this end, in *Luttrell*,[4] the Court of Appeal cited with approval the test laid down by the Supreme Court of South Australia in the case of the *R v Bonython*.[5] Here it was established that there were two questions that needed to be asked by a trial judge in determining whether an expert is to be heard:

(i) The first is whether the subject matter of the opinion falls within the class of subjects upon which expert testimony is permissible.
    This may be divided into two parts:
  (a) Whether the subject matter of the opinion is such that a person without instruction or experience in the area of knowledge or human experience would be able to form a sound judgment on the matter without the assistance of witnesses possessing special knowledge or experience in the area
  (b) Whether the subject matter of the opinion forms part of a body of knowledge or experience which is sufficiently organised or recognised to be accepted as a reliable body of knowledge or experience, a special acquaintance with which by the witness would render his opinion of assistance to the court

(ii) The second question is whether the witness has acquired by study or experience sufficient knowledge of the subject to render his opinion of value in resolving the issues before the court.

Although the courts have been relatively consistent in the need for quality control, abstract references to concepts such as 'sound judgment' and 'reliability' are very much subjective and likely to vary according to the experience and understanding of the individual judge. Although there is no specific Northern Ireland case law on the issue, it is widely accepted that the same rules apply. While the Criminal Procedure Rules were amended in 2014 to provide for a much more robust 'gatekeeping' role for the judge in England and Wales to determine whether the evidence concerned was deemed to be sufficiently reliable to be put before the jury,[6] no such rules have been introduced as yet in Northern Ireland.

For the most part, expert evidence is regarded as unproblematic where it pertains to the traditional academic sciences, though the rapid pace at which forensics and technology are constantly advancing means that new fields of study are developing, and what may be considered 'good science' for now may be questioned or debunked in the near future. There is little doubt that expert evidence is being called with greater frequency, which carries obvious implications for both the costs and duration of proceedings, with an estimate that around 3% of the legal aid budget is now spent on experts' fees.[7] Indeed, so extensive is the range of issues on which experts might now be called to comment that it would be impossible to devise any sort of exhaustive list; at the time of writing, the UK Register of Expert Witnesses has currently more than 17,000 entries in its subject list. As the range of fields of expertise continues to expand, questions are rightly being asked about when it is necessary to have an 'expert' give a view to the court. As in England and Wales, the decision on admissibility will ultimately lie with the trial judge, although practice in Northern Ireland would indicate that it is highly unusual for a judge to exclude such evidence of his or her own motion. In general terms, the adversarial model of proof dictates that judges will generally leave the presentation of the case to the parties and will usually only exclude evidence in circumstances where a meritorious application to do so is made.

5.2 The Reception of Expert Evidence

The only statutory provisions specific to the use of expert evidence in criminal proceedings are found in the Crown Court (NI) Rules 1979 and Magistrates' Court Rules (NI) 1984. However, aside from these very particular stipulations relating to the adducing expert evidence in support of special measures applications,[8] and the generic disclosure provisions contained in the Criminal Procedure and Investigations Act 1996, no further statutory regulation applies. The most authoritative practitioner's text in the jurisdiction, *Valentine's Criminal Procedure*, provides that the 'rules as to opinion, expert opinion and impression evidence are the same as in civil actions'.[9] This essentially means that all expert evidence in Northern Ireland's criminal and civil courts is governed by the Rules of the Court of Judicature (Northern Ireland) 1980, where Order 38 outlines a number of general rules relating to evidence which apply to expert evidence. For example, under Order 38 1B, unless the court agrees otherwise, the number of expert witnesses that may be called by any one party to give oral evidence shall be limited to two medical experts and one other expert of any kind.

The remainder of the law relating to expert evidence is governed by common law, most of which has evolved through the English courts. As a starting point, it is for the court to determine whether expert evidence is required at all; this reflects the position of the leading English cases of *DPP v A and BC Chewing Gum* (1968) 1 QB 159 and *Turner* (1975) 1 All ER 70, where it was held that when a particular issue does not require specialist knowledge, an expert should not be called and the matter should be left entirely to the jury. Thus, where a particular matter falls within the knowledge and experience of the jury, or where it concerns an issue of human nature and behaviour within the limits of normality, expert evidence will not be admissible. In *R v Calderwood* (1983) 10 NIJB, two paramilitaries were charged with murder. One called psychiatric evidence as part of his defence, which was deemed to be admissible only so far as it was relevant to his intelligence quotient; it could not be taken into account in assessing the accused's susceptibility to duress as the court held that duress was to be determined by ordinary standards where there is no evidence of mental abnormality. This position was affirmed by the Northern Irish Crown Court in the more recent case of *R v Chang Hai Zhangi* (2008) NICC 5, where it was stated that the core function of expert evidence was 'to provide the court and the jury with information which is likely to be outside the experience and knowledge of a judge and jury'.[10]

Evidence of mental states, including emotions, is regarded as unsuitable for expert comment unless the accused is suffering from a recognised medical condition that impacts upon the state of mind. While there have been no recent cases on the issues before the Northern Ireland courts, the English authorities are again instructive. Thus, in *Hegarty* (1994) Crim. LR 353, the Court of Appeal stated that questions of emotional instability were not suitable for expert comment; in *R v Weightman* (1991) 92 Cr. App. R. 291, a psychiatrist's evidence concerning the impact of stress upon the defendant was deemed inadmissible, while in *R v Browning* (1991) 94 Cr. App. R. 109 a psychologist was not permitted to testify as to the likely extent of memory loss in a 'normal' witness. Even where the accused may have an abnormal personality trait, this will not justify admission where he or she is within the normal IQ range and is not suffering from a recognised medical condition (see *Masih* [1986] Crim. LR 395).

5.3 Duties of the Expert Witness

One of the most pressing critiques of the adversary model is that the principle of free proof dictates that experts will generally support the case of the party that calls them. This tends to contradict the widely held notion that an expert's primary duty is towards the court, rather than to the party calling them. While this principle is enshrined in England and Wales within the Criminal Procedure Rules,[11] a Northern Ireland Practice Direction[12] states that it stems from the common law and cites with approval the specific duties set out by Cresswell J in *Compania Naviera SA v Prudential Assurance Company Limited (the Ikarian Reefer)* [1993] 2 Lloyds Reports 68 at 81:

1. Expert evidence presented to the Court should be and should be seen to be the independent product of the expert uninfluenced as to form or content by the exigencies of litigation. …
2. An expert witness should provide independent assistance to the Court by way of objective unbiased opinion in relation to matters within his expertise. … An expert witness in the High Court should never assume the role of advocate.
3. An expert witness should state the facts or assumptions on which his opinion is based. He should not omit to consider material facts which detract from his concluded opinion. …
4. An expert witness should make it clear when a particular question or issue falls outside his expertise.
5. If an expert's opinion is not properly researched because he considers that insufficient data is available then this must be stated with an indication that the opinion is no more than a provisional one. …
6. If after exchange of reports, an expert witness changes his view on a material matter … such change of view should be communicated … to the other side without delay and when appropriate to the Court.
7. Where expert evidence refers to photographs, plans, calculations … survey reports or other similar documents these must be provided to the opposite party at the same time as the exchange of reports. …

In addition to proffering an objective opinion, the expert is under a further duty to state the facts or assumptions upon which that opinion is based,[13] and should inform the court if he or she did not have the necessary level of expertise within a particular area or if there is insufficient evidence on which to express an opinion.[14] If an expert fails to understand this duty to the court, then he or she should be debarred from giving evidence.[15] Experts may, however, cite the findings or research by others in their field as a basis for their opinions; there is no requirement that any direct evidence be submitted to the court. Ultimately, if the source on which the expert is relying appears to the court to be especially weak or overly speculative, there is nothing to prevent the judge excluding it under Article 76 of the Police and Criminal Evidence (NI) Order (which parallels section 78 of the English legislation through providing for a discretionary exclusion to exclude evidence that would be unfair to the accused) or at common law pursuant to *R v Sang* (1980) AC 402.

5.4 Restrictions on the Scope of Expert Opinion

Experts are permitted to give evidence relating to any matters falling within their expertise,[16] but must strictly confine their opinions to matters that fall within their professional competence. Moreover, the increasingly diverse range of matters that may lend themselves to expert testimony highlights the fact that the courts must take steps to ensure that all who purport to be experts have a sufficient level of competency in their fields. In the traditional fields, such as medicine, engineering and accountancy, membership of a recognised professional association will generally suffice. The Council for the Registration of Forensic Practitioners has maintained a database of competent practitioners in 13 specified fields throughout the UK, and plans are currently under consideration for a similar registration scheme for forensic psychologists.[17]

However, this is not the case with all disciplines, and indeed there is some controversy as to whether the skills of some of the experts who testify have any scientific basis at all. As fields of study expand yet become more specialised, it may be necessary, on occasion, for 'quasi-experts' to be called who hold no formal qualifications. While reported cases from the Northern Irish courts are rare, it is assumed they would adopt a similar approach to the English courts on such matters. For example, in *R v Clare and Peach* (1995) 2 Cr. App. R. 333, a police officer had undertaken a prolonged study of a poor-quality video-recording in order to gauge what precisely was happening in the footage. Although he had no personal qualifications in reading such footage or facial mapping (see below), the court held that his experience in watching the video some 40 times in slow motion had qualified him to make expert comment. In *Hodges* (2003) 2 Cr. App. R. 15, a police officer was regarded as an expert on the nature of the black market for heroin in a particular area, while in *Dallagher* (2003) 1 Cr. App. R. 195, a Dutch police officer was deemed to have sufficient experience in identifying ear prints, even though he held no forensic qualifications. Here the English Court of Appeal agreed that his evidence was rightly admitted as ear print identification was a new and emerging field of forensics with little consensus in the scientific community. The decision, which was made through the application of the 'ordinary tests of relevance and reliability', has, however, been criticised on the grounds that forensic science, by its very nature, demands to be subjected to a specialist and scientific standard, rather than that used by the courts to receive non-specialist evidence.[18]

However, even in novel and emerging fields, there has been a marked reluctance of the appellate courts to intervene where the scientific credibility of the witness is contentious. In *R v Luttrell* (2004) 2 Cr. App. R. 31, the prosecution called a lip-reading expert to state what she felt a group of men captured on CCTV images had been discussing. At the time of the trial, the expertise required to lip-read from televised evidence was such a specialised area that there were apparently only four other experts in the United Kingdom who would have been capable of giving such evidence. The appellant's argument that lip-reading in such circumstances had never been shown to be reliable (and should therefore have been inadmissible) was rejected by the court. Noting that it was 'entirely appropriate' for the level of expertise to be challenged in court in order to establish the credibility of the expert, the court stated that trawling through the track record of the witness should not be repeated at subsequent trials. In something of an ironic twist, at another trial shortly afterwards, the defence was able to illustrate significant weaknesses in the same expert's qualifications and training; shortly afterwards, the Crown Prosecution Service (CPS) announced that it was reviewing all files in which H had been involved and would not be calling her again.[19]

Lip-reading is just one field of expertise that has been regarded with some degree of suspicion; other relatively novel and narrow fields within the realm of science and medicine have been similarly questioned. These have included the existence of Gulf War syndrome and battered women syndrome. Some concerns have been raised in respect of the use of voice identification techniques; in *R v O'Doherty* (2002) NI 263, the Northern Ireland Court of Appeal quashed a conviction based largely on a detective's recognition of the voice of the male caller to ambulance control as that of the applicant. Noting that 'time had moved on' since the earlier English decision in *R v Robb* (1991) 93 Cr. App. R. 161, the court held that such auditory identification was generally unreliable unless supported by acoustic analysis. Nicholson LJ added that such cases required a suitable warning be issued to the jury in all cases involving voice identification evidence, though he added that the nature and extent of such a warning would depend upon the particular circumstances of individual cases.

There have been similar levels of unease surrounding the use of so-called 'low copy' DNA evidence, which tends to be adduced when samples found at a crime scene are not large enough to be analysed through conventional scientific analysis. Instead, copies are made of the original sample until it can be usefully analysed. The perceived problem with this technique is that if the original sample was in any way damaged or contaminated, the copies produced from it will also be damaged in a similar fashion. This risk was acknowledged by the Northern Ireland Crown Court in *R v Sean Hoey* (2007) NICC 49, where the applicant faced 58 counts relating to terrorism including the murder of 29 people in the Omagh bomb atrocity in 1998. In dismissing the case against Hoey, Mr Justice Weir expressed concerns over the 'validation of the science and methodology associated with (it)'.

Following the ruling, the use of the technique was suspended in the UK pending a CPS review, which eventually concluded that the service 'had not seen anything to suggest that any current problems exist with LCN'. As such, the suspension was lifted and the technique endorsed by the English Court of Appeal in *R v Reed and Reed; Garmson* (2009) EWCA Crim. 2698, where it was held that not only should low copy DNA be admissible, but that challenges to the validity of the scientific method should no longer be permitted where the amount of genetic material was above the stochastic threshold (which the court determined to be 200 picograms). However, it was added that juries should also evaluate the DNA evidence and it should not form the sole basis of a conviction, but should rather be considered in the context of the evidence as a whole. The technique was also given tacit approval by the Northern Ireland courts in *R v Duffy and Shivers* (2012) NICC 1 (concerning the dissident Republican attack at Masserene Army Barracks in March 2009). While both defendants were ultimately acquitted (Duffy at the original trial and Shivers at a retrial ([2013] NICC 10), the modified technique of low template DNA was accepted by the court as providing evidence linking both defendants to the vehicle used in the attack.

5.5 Procedure and Advance Notification

The procedural aspects of expert evidence are governed by the Crown Court (Advance Notice of Expert Evidence) Rules (Northern Ireland) 1989 and the Magistrates' Court (Advance Notice of Expert Evidence) Rules (Northern Ireland) 1997. These instruments provide that any party wishing to adduce expert evidence either of fact or opinion must adduce a copy of a written statement containing the expert findings as soon as is practicable. If a party has reasonable grounds for believing that such disclosure might lead to the expert being intimidated, that party is not obliged to comply with this requirement so long as written notice is provided to all other parties to that effect. Any party seeking to adduce expert evidence without complying with these requirements can do so only with the leave of the court.

The Criminal Procedure and Investigation Act 1996 applies to Northern Ireland in so far as it governs disclosure obligations of expert witnesses. As such, under Section 3(1), the prosecutor must disclose to the defence any material upon which the prosecution is not relying and which is capable of undermining the case for the prosecution or assisting the defence. In *Duffy and Shivers* (above), the prosecution obtained a crime analyst's report from the crime scene. The analyst had been instructed to examine the possibility that the height of the masked gunmen captured in CCTV matched that of Duffy. His findings were that the two gunmen were 6 feet 3 inches and 6 feet

6 inches, whereas Duffy was only 5 feet 11 inches. Because this material did not assist the prosecution case, they chose not to rely upon it. However, in line with their disclosure obligations a copy of the report was forwarded to the defence, who then chose to call the analyst as their own defence witness. It can be noted, however, that there is no corresponding obligation on the defence to disclose their own expert reports to the prosecution.

In practice, in summary prosecutions, prosecution expert evidence will be served on the defence with all other prosecution statements of evidence in the form of a court summons served on the defendant either before the initial hearing or alternatively during an early remand appearance. In cases proceeding on indictment, expert evidence will be served at the Magistrates' Court prior to any preliminary inquiry that determines whether or not there is a case to answer (i.e., a prima facie case) before the matter is sent to the Crown Court. In both cases, defence experts are generally not instructed until all prosecution evidence has been served. The rationale for this position is that the defence needs to know the nature of the evidence to be challenged prior to incurring the expense of obtaining an expert report.

Section 6D of the Criminal Procedures and Investigations Act 1996 (inserted via the Criminal Justice Act 2003) requires any accused to provide a prosecutor with the name and address of any expert that he intended to instruct. However, while this provision applies in England and Wales and was intended to be extended to Northern Ireland, it has still not been brought into effect. One possible reason for the delay is that Section 6D is linked to Section 6C (similarly not enacted), which provides that the names and addresses of all defence witnesses be provided to the prosecution in advance of trial. Given the unique political landscape in Northern Ireland, and ongoing concerns about the nature and extent of witness intimidation (notwithstanding the peace process), it may have been felt that any introduction of the rules may bring with it unnecessary security concerns.

5.6 Single Joint Experts

It has become increasingly commonplace for criminal justice systems to provide some form of incentives to agree on a single court-appointed expert which should ordinarily result in substantial cost savings. Recent years have seen this practice become more frequent in civil cases in Northern Ireland, and it is also widely used in English criminal cases where multiple defendants wish to rely on expert evidence.[20] However, no equivalent provision is made for criminal practice in Northern Ireland where it is usual practice for both sides to rely on their own experts.[21] However, the Northern Ireland Law Commission has sought to encourage the use of joint experts in multiple defendant criminal cases, and in a 2016 consultation document, *Examining the Use of Expert Witnesses Appearing in the Courts in Northern Ireland*,[22] the Department of Justice has asked for views on how effectively the approach has operated in the civil sphere and how it might be made to work more effectively in criminal cases.[23] It is unclear, however, whether these moves are likely to impact practice in the short term as there are fears that any interference of the defence's ability to appoint its own expert could conceivably interfere with fair trial rights under Article 6(3)(d) of the European Convention (namely, the defendant's right to be able to effectively challenge the prosecution evidence).

5.7 Expert Evidence and Hearsay

Article 10 of the Criminal Justice (Evidence) (Northern Ireland) Order 1988 (replicating Section 30(1) of the Criminal Justice Act 1988) states that an expert report shall be admissible as evidence in criminal proceedings, whether or not the person making it attends to give oral evidence in those proceedings. It is further provided that in the event that the person making the report shall not give oral evidence, the report shall only be admissible with the leave of the court. Therefore, where an expert is called as a witness at trial, his or her report is admissible without leave as an exception to the hearsay rule. Where the expert does not attend, then the court's leave to use the report is required. Moreover, in advancing their opinions, experts are not curtailed by the hearsay rule to the same extent as non-expert witnesses. Thus, pursuant to Article 31 of the Criminal Justice (Evidence) (Northern Ireland) Order 2004, it is perfectly permissible for an expert to rely on the findings of a colleague or a member of staff, and Article 22(1)(8) also preserves any rule of law under which in criminal proceedings an expert witness may draw on the body of expertise relevant to his field.

5.8 Law Reform in Northern Ireland

The rules in England and Wales governing the use of expert evidence were considerably refined by the 2014 amendments to the Criminal Procedure Rules, which were adopted in light of the recommendations by the Law Commission in their 2011 report, *Expert Evidence in Criminal Proceedings in England and Wales*.[24] While the recommendations were made specifically for the English jurisdiction, and resulted in no changes to the legal framework in Northern Ireland, the changes have undoubtedly acted as a catalyst in prompting discussion about the need for reform in Northern Ireland. In

September 2011, the Northern Ireland *Access to Justice Review* recommended that 'the Department of Justice allocates a dedicated resource to the development and implementation of a strategy for securing expert witness evidence for the courts on a basis that secures value for money, consulting with stakeholders as appropriate'.[25] In addressing this recommendation, the review suggested that consideration should be given to:

(a) The process by which the need for added value from expert evidence is identified and by which experts are appointed – and the circumstances where one independent expert appointed by the court would meet the requirements of justice (as opposed to experts being appointed by each party)
(b) A framework of fixed fees to be paid for experts in publicly funded cases, taking account of market conditions and fee levels set in England and Wales
(c) The arrangements for remunerating experts in legally aided cases in a timely fashion
(d) The development of registers of suitably qualified experts – working with the law society and other jurisdictions
(e) The use of video links, IT and written reports to reduce the costs associated with securing expert evidence from outside the jurisdiction
(f) Liaising with other jurisdictions in the United Kingdom and with the Republic of Ireland to develop complementary policies and systems on these matters
(g) The recoverability of the costs of experts as between the parties and ensuring that the legal aid fund is not unduly exposed

As part of a package of reforms to the legal aid budget, the minister of justice subsequently instigated a 'Legal Aid Expert Witness' project, which forms the basis for the recent consultation document, *Examining the Use of Expert Witnesses Appearing in the Courts in Northern Ireland*, noted above. More specifically, the department outlined plans to address problems relating to the 'designated competence' of experts, whereby it becomes apparent in the course of investigations that an expert has insufficient expertise to proffer an opinion on the matter, thus necessitating a second expert to be instructed. It was noted that such a situation may lead to situations where multiple experts are instructed in the same case, and where parties will seek to involve new experts where the original report does not provide strong enough support for a client's case. In view of the department, the tendency to make use of multiple experts in this way means that 'the value for money test is not met', rendering the process both 'wasteful and … unsustainable'.[26] The outcome of the consultation remains to be seen, and it is uncertain how policymakers might seek to operationalise the proposal.

A second significant issue highlighted in the consultation document relates to the apparent need for a centralised register of expert witnesses. Currently, Northern Ireland practitioners locate experts from a wide range of organisations which maintain their own databases or registers of experts. Many of these, including the Society of Expert Witnesses, the Academy of Experts, the Expert Witness Institute, the UK Register of Expert Witnesses and the Council for the Regulation of Forensic Practitioners, are UK-wide, and it is not unusual for experts based in other parts of the UK to testify in Northern Ireland courts. Databases specific to Northern Ireland include ExpertWitnessNI, which provides a list of experts in the fields of children and family litigation. This is essentially a register of experts in the fields of psychology, social work, paediatrics and psychiatry which can be searched through an electronic database maintained by the bar library. An online expert dictionary also exists. The consultation document proposes an option of a centralised register which might impose a requirement for all registered experts to undertake legally aided work, though it is conceded that an 'unintended consequence' might be that the pool of experts available to testify in the courts would be significantly reduced. Again, it is uncertain at the time of writing as to whether the department might eventually proceed with this proposal; much will depend upon the nature of the responses gathered during the consultation process.

A third proposal highlighted in the consultation document is the potential for costs to be reduced through increasing the use of video-link technology to receive expert testimony. Acknowledging that technology is already widely used, the document canvasses views as to how current practice might be improved and whether a presumption should be put in place to the effect that evidence by experts from outside the jurisdiction should ordinarily be received through video link.

5.9 Concluding Comments

During the years of the 'Troubles', expert evidence featured prominently in the criminal courts, where ballistics, explosives and forensics experts were regularly called upon to testify in so-called 'Diplock' proceedings relating to scheduled offences.[27] While there has been a welcome decline in these types of cases since the paramilitary ceasefires of 1994, the reliance on expert evidence seems set to increase in future years as technology and forensic science advance into new fields. As the other chapters in this volume attest, the various conundrums concerning whether (and how) expertise ought to be assessed by the courts, and whether moves towards the use of single joint experts are fair to the accused, are largely the same across the various UK jurisdictions and beyond. As the twin vicissitudes of austerity and managerialism continue to shape the evolution of evidential and procedural rules, changes to the funding regime will almost certainly mean increased incentives for parties to minimise the use of multiple experts. However, far-reaching reform to the substantial legal rules governing the reception of expert evidence remains an unlikely prospect for Northern Ireland in the short term.

Notes

1. *R v Silverlock* (1894) 2 QB 766.
2. (2013) EWCA Crim. 2.
3. Ibid., at para. 11.
4. (2004) 2 Cr. App. R. 31.
5. (1984) 38 SASR 45.
6. See r. 33A(5), which was based on the recommendations of the Law Commission in its 2011 report, *Expert Evidence in Criminal Proceedings in England and Wales*, Report No. 325 (London: HMSO).
7. Department of Justice for Northern Ireland, *Examining the Use of Expert Witnesses Appearing in the Courts in Northern Ireland* (Belfast: Department of Justice, 2014).
8. See Magistrates' Court Rules (NI) 1984, r. 149AH and Crown Court (NI) Rules 1979, r. 44CF.
9. Valentine, [12.118].
10. This case was unsuccessfully appealed to the Court of Appeal (2011) NICA 25 on separate grounds but no dispute was taken by either party or indeed by the Court of Appeal itself with regards to the principle established in *Calderwood* subsequently affirmed in the Crown Court.
11. Rule 33(2).
12. Commercial List Practice Direction No. 6/2002. Available: https://www.courtsni.gov.uk/en-GB/Judicial%20Decisions/Practice%20Directions/Documents/Practice%20Direction%206%20of%202002/j_j_PD%206-2002.pdf.
13. *The Ikarian Reefer* [1993] FSR 563.
14. Ibid.
15. *Stevens v Gullis* [2000] 1 All ER 527.
16. Valentine, [12.120].
17. See Department of Health, *Applied Psychology: Enhancing Public Protection* (London: HMSO, 2005).
18. See O'Brian, W., 'Scrutiny of Expert Evidence: Recent Decisions Highlight the Tensions' (2003) 7 *E & P* 172.
19. See further Jackson, S., 'Read MY Lips' (2004) 154 *New Law Journal* 1146.
20. Criminal Procedure Rules, r. 33.7.
21. Under Order 40 of the Rules of the Court of Judicature (Northern Ireland) 1980 (which governs the use of experts in both civil and criminal cases), a court may of its own motion or on the application of any party appoint an independent expert or if necessary two or more experts to inquire and report upon any question of fact or opinion not involving questions of law or of construction.

22. See n.7.
23. Ibid. at para. [4.6]–[4.7].
24. See n.6.
25. Department of Justice for Northern Ireland, *Access to Justice Review* (Belfast: Department of Justice), para. 5.15.1.
26. Ibid., para. 4.2.
27. 'Diplock' proceedings involved a judge sitting alone without a jury owning the high risk of juror intimidation. In place since 1973, they were abolished following the enactment of the Justice and Security (Northern Ireland) Act 2007. However, non-jury trials can still take place in Northern Ireland, if any of the conditions in Section 1 of the act are met.

Responsibilities and Obligations of the Expert Witness

6

DAME SUE BLACK AND
NIAMH NIC DAÉID

Contents

6.1 Introduction

It may appear like linguistic semantics, but there is an important distinction between the responsibilities and the obligations of an expert witness. Responsibilities are intrinsic to the individual and inherent within them is an ethical or moral duty for them to be addressed through the spirit of sound intention. Despite the fact that responsibilities are rarely mandated by law or authority, a person may still be held to account should they abrogate what society deems to be either their moral or ethical responsibility (Edwards 1969;

Haji 2016). In contrast, an obligation is formally mandated and may be morally, socially or legally binding. An obligation may be imposed by society, law or conscience and the practitioner is bound or restricted by such requirements (Edwards 1969). In its simplest concept, a responsibility is something that a civilised society considers that one 'should' do, while an obligation is something that one 'must' do. In relation to the role of the expert witness, then it is the *responsibility* of the individual practitioner to ensure that they uphold the *obligations* against which they, as a professional, must practice their craft. It is the responsibility of the expert witness to know that such obligations exist and to ensure that they remain current in their understanding should the obligations change. It is the responsibility of the expert witness to understand in detail the obligations by which they must operate and to appreciate that they will be held to account should they be either unable or unwilling to fulfil them. They must therefore accept and expect that a contravention of obligations may impact on their ability to continue to practice as an expert witness

The obligations of the expert witness are very clearly set out in Part 19 of the Criminal Procedure Rules (2015) for England and Wales. The obligations surrounding expert witness evidence in Scotland are somewhat more vague but largely follow those in England and Wales with requirements for corroboration being the principal difference (Criminal Procedure [Scotland] Act 1995; [Crown Office and Procurator Fiscal Service COPFS] 2015). This section concentrates more heavily on those clearly mandated by the judicial system in England and Wales and assumes that expert witnesses in other parts of the United Kingdom might consider it their responsibility to recognise the value of these obligations as sound practice to follow within their own jurisdiction. It should be noted that the obligations incumbent upon the expert witness are only those mandated as statutory instruments within the Criminal Procedure Rules (2015), while other literature, including that of the Crown Prosecution Service (CPS) in the booklet 'Guidance on Expert Evidence' (2014), the Forensic Science Regulator's information sheet on 'Legal Obligations' (2015) and the British Medical Association's 'Expert Witness Guidance' (2007), are interpretations of the mandated obligations and as such, their role is primarily to provide guidance for the practitioner to enable them to understand fully their legal obligations. It should also be noted that the Criminal Procedure Rules (2015) postdate the documentation from the CPS (2014), the Forensic Science Regulator (2015) and the BMA (2007), which all refer to Rule 33 within the Criminal Procedure Rules (2014) or the Criminal Procedure Rules (2005).

Part 19 of the Criminal Procedure Rules (2015) are laid out as nine rules and headed as 'Expert Evidence'.

6.2 Expert Evidence

6.2.1 Rule 19.1 p149 CPR (2015)

These few introductory lines highlight that Part 19 of the Criminal Procedure Rules (CPR) should be applied when it is the intention of a legal party to introduce expert opinion evidence. It is important to appreciate that the rules are formulated for the senior courts of England and Wales and the Magistrates' Courts in England and Wales and are not drafted for the expert witness. The section confirms that an expert refers to 'a person who is required to give or prepare expert evidence for the purpose of criminal proceedings, including evidence required to determine fitness to plead of the purposes of sentencing'. The CPS guidance booklet (2014) offers the definition that 'an expert witness is a witness who provides to the court a statement of opinion on any admissible matter calling for expertise by the witness and is qualified to give such an opinion'.

This part of the CPR (2015) is therefore directed specifically to the legal teams and therefore poses the following questions – When is an expert an expert, and how should they recognise that they are qualified to give such an opinion? See later in this section for a discussion of the topic of accreditation of expert witnesses.

6.2.2 Rule 19.2 p149 CPR (2015)

In three sections, this part considers the *expert's duty to the court.*

Section 1 informs that the expert is to help the court to achieve its overriding objective and to do this through giving an opinion that is both objective and unbiased but is within the expert's area, or areas, of expertise. The expert witness is expected to assist the court in fulfilling its duty to case management and to do so by complying with the directions made by the court and to inform the court of any significant failure in such an objective. The duty of providing unbiased and objective testimony answers only to the overriding duty of the court and does not lie with the party from whom the expert witness received instruction. The expert witness is a witness to the court and while they may appear in court as an expert witness for the Crown or for the defence, their obligation is to give impartial and unbiased evidence to the court and not to be influenced or swayed by either legal team or the investigative authority who may have initially engaged their services. This overriding obligation to the court is addressed in Section 2 of this rule.

Section 3 of this rule obliges the expert witness to define their area, or areas, of expertise in their report and again when giving evidence in person. The expert is obliged when giving evidence in person to draw to the attention of the court any matter that is not within their area of expertise and also to inform *all* parties and the court if their opinion should change from that expressed within the original report. The 'Legal Obligations' publication from the Forensic Science Regulator (2015) gives some valuable criminal case references where each aspect of this part of the CPR (2015) can be further researched. The regulator's publication extends further than the CPR (2015) stance, including that the witness must state facts and assumptions upon which their opinion is based; the expert should be clear when the opinion is not properly researched, is provisional or is controversial; the expert should indicate where a range of opinion exists; the expert should disclose circumstances that might give rise to a conflict of interest; and the witness must not assume the role of advocate or jury. These are all sound advice to ensure that the final report has the greatest probative value to the court.

6.2.3 Rule 19.3 p149 CPR (2015)

This rule relates to the *introduction of expert evidence* and has four sections. It addresses the processes and procedures that the legal teams should follow if their intention is to introduce expert evidence in the case. This section has little direct bearing on the expert witness other than perhaps in Section 4b, where it is stated that unless otherwise agreed or the court directs, a party may not 'introduce in evidence an expert report if the expert does not give evidence in person'. Therefore, while not every expert who writes a report will give evidence in court, they should assume that the act of writing a report may result in them being cited to give evidence in person.

6.2.4 Rule 19.4 p150 CPR (2015)

This rule relates to the *content of the expert's report*. There are 11 sections to this rule and they are labelled from a to k inclusive, and this is perhaps the most pertinent area of the Criminal Procedure Rules (2015) for the expert to address as they are mandatory and they outline what the courts expect the witness to include in their written report.

1. The expert must detail their qualifications, their relevant experience and their accreditation. The rule states 'must', and therefore it is germane that any person who presents as an expert must be able to evidence what makes them so and who has certified that it is indeed so. The aim is to ensure that the court only hears evidence from those who are sufficiently knowledgeable in their area of expertise and does not permit access to those who are 'little more than enthusiastic amateurs' (CPS 2014: 7).
2. The expert must give details of any literature or other information that they have relied upon while writing their report. Published

literature permits the court to understand the wider concept of the opinion reached.

3. The expert must contain a statement in their report that sets out the substance of all facts given to them which are material to the opinions that they express in their report and upon which their opinion was based. This information may come from the investigative agencies, the legal teams or other expert witnesses where the results of their investigation may have a bearing on the opinion reached by the expert. Think, for example, of a reporting scientist in a laboratory who may undertake the bench-work analysis and then pass these results to the expert witness such that their original laboratory work will be core to the formulation of the expert's opinion.
4. The expert must be clear on which of the facts stated in their report are within their own area(s) of expertise and knowledge. This is an area where the expert may be tempted to express an opinion that is not within their professional expertise and they must state clearly in both their report and when giving evidence in person when a matter is not within their area of knowledge.
5. The expert must say who carried out any examination, measurement, test or experiment and state the qualifications, relevant experience and accreditation of that person, saying whether the work was carried out under the expert's supervision or not, and the expert must summarise the findings upon which they rely. This overlaps with section c above, as another practitioner may also convey information that is relevant to the final opinion given.
6. The expert must inform if there is a range of opinion on the matters addressed within the report and give reasons as to why they reached their opinion, bearing in mind that other outcomes might have been possible.
7. If the expert is not able to give an opinion without qualification, then they must state their qualification.
8. The expert must include such information as required by the court to be able to decide whether their opinion is suitably reliable to be admitted as evidence.
9. The expert must include a summary of their conclusions reached.
10. The expert must contain a statement within their report that conveys the expert's understanding of their duty to the court and that they have complied with the duties required and will continue to do so. Such statements vary in their wording, but documents such as CPS (2014) offer templates that can be considered.
11. The expert's report must also contain a declaration as to the truth of the witness statement. Templates for this declaration are also available in a number of documents, including CPS (2014).

It is clear therefore that the 'rules' provide quite detailed guidance to the expert witness as to the required format and content of their report, but further helpful suggestions are to be found in the Forensic Science Regulator's document on legal obligations (2015).

6.2.5 Rule 19.5 p151 CPR (2015)

The expert must be informed at once by a legal party when their report has been served on another party.

6.2.6 Rule 19.6 p151 CPR (2015)

There are four sections to this rule which addresses *pre-hearing discussion of expert evidence*. This rule applies when more than one party intends to introduce expert witness evidence and the court may direct the experts to form a common statement identifying the areas where they agree and those where they disagree. This is a ruling for England and Wales and is not one that is followed in the Scottish courts, where any differences between experts are more commonly addressed in the courtroom.

6.2.7 Rules 19.7 p152 and 19.8 p152 CPR (2015)

These rules address where a single joint expert report is directed by the court, and again this is not a process followed in the Scottish courts. The expert may be selected from a prepared list if the co-defendants cannot agree on a common expert. Rule 19.8 is focused on the responsibility for payment of a single expert as each party is jointly, and severally, liable for payment of fees and expenses.

6.2.8 Rule 19.9 p152 CPR (2015)

This rule relates to the court's power to vary requirements in relation to time limits and potential extensions through delay.

6.3 Disclosure

Disclosure is one of the most important issues in the criminal justice system, and it is addressed in Part 15 of the Criminal Procedure Rules (2015). This is an area in which the expert witness also has important obligations and it is essential that requirements are understood fully (CPS 2010). Full disclosure by the Crown to the defence is in accordance with Article 6 of the European Convention of Human Rights (Council of Europe 2010). This refers to the right to a fair trial, which is the fundamental precept of the oldest surviving legal document, the Magna Carta. A fair trial is predicated on all parties having access to all information relating to the charges brought and hence the core precept of full disclosure by the party that brings the charge against the accused.

If a breach occurs in relation to disclosure, then it can result in a prosecution being halted or delayed, a conviction being quashed on appeal, adverse comment about the expert witness and professional embarrassment, which could include action against the expert witness by their professional body. There is the potential for civil action by an accused and the practitioner may lose their accreditation (COPFS 2015).

There are four obligations to be discharged by the expert in relation to disclosure, and they are easy to remember as retain, record, reveal and review.

Retain – The simple obligation for the expert witness here is that *everything* should be retained. The expert witness is not permitted to decide what is important and what is not, as everything pertinent to the case in hand should be retained. Retention is until informed otherwise, and depending upon the nature of the case this may be for many years.

Record – The recording of information commences at the moment the expert receives instruction and will persist throughout the life span of the case. Records are required to be kept of the collection and movement of items which include dates, names, means of passing material, etc. Notes should be signed and dated and of sufficient detail that an additional expert may follow the logic of the progress of the work. Notes should be kept of every meeting attended and of telephone conversations. Points of agreement or disagreement need to recorded, and all electronic records such as emails must be retained. All case notes should be constructed in such a way as to facilitate review. All updates or comments should be clearly outlined. It is accepted, though, that not all material will be used in an investigation and there are guidelines as to how unused material is disclosed (CPS 2010).

Reveal – Again the concept here is very simple. The expert must reveal *everything*. This may be revealed to the legal teams either through (a) the expert's report, (b) formal statements or (c) an index of unused material. The CPS (2010) guidance on disclosure includes appendices that may be used as templates for recording an index of unused material, declaration statements and the expert witness's self-certificate.

Review – The expert witness should review their conclusions if any new information becomes available either before or after a trial or an appeal (Association of Chief Police Officers in Scotland 2010; COPFS 2015).

The expert witness must also be familiar with the legal obligations relating to exhibits (called productions in Scotland). The legislation for this lies within the Police and Criminal Evidence Act 1984 (PACE). The obligations here can be linked very clearly to the requirements outlined in CPR (2015) in relation to the construction of the expert witness report and following the principles outlined above in the 'record' approach to disclosure.

6.4 Summary

The obligations of the expert witness are therefore relatively clear:

1. Assist the court to perform its duties in a manner that is objective and unbiased.
2. Produce a report that evidences your suitability to be an expert witness, details your activities and justifies your opinion as an expert witness.
3. Do not stray outside your area of expertise.
4. Inform all parties if your opinions change.
5. Retain, record, reveal and review all opinions.

It is important to remember that the expert witness is only an expert witness when the court accepts them as such (COPFS 2015).

6.5 Accreditation

Accreditation is a process whereby the competency, credibility or authority of an organisation or an individual is certified by an external body or agency against an accepted standard. Organisations which offer an accreditation service must themselves be certified externally to do so. Within the forensic science domain, the accreditation provider is normally a national accreditation agency which (generally) offers accreditation to organisations rather than individual practitioners.

The terminology relating to accreditation and the setting of standards is by nature precise; however, there is an occasional tendency to interchange 'certification' of individual practitioners with 'accreditation' of such practitioners and the two are quite different. Generally speaking, certification *may be* provided by professional bodies through their own processes, often without the requirement of external involvement or review (although many professional bodies will have external input), whereas accreditation can only be awarded by organisations which have the mandate and certification to accredit.

The accreditation process for organisations involves the inspection and assessment of both written material, including quality manuals, standard operating procedures, staff training and competency records, and other documentation which demonstrates the organisation's compliance to the specific standard against which they are being assessed. Accreditation standards are generally set formally by internationally accepted organisations such as the International Organization for Standardization (ISO) but can also be generated by regulatory bodies such that the standards comply with the requirements of overarching ISO standards.

An organisation which achieves accreditation is expected to be able to demonstrate their abilities in delivering their services in a way that is impartial and reliable, meets the standards against which they are assessed and provides a measure of confidence in the quality of the service they deliver.

The accreditation process usually involves a set of specific stages:

A pre-assessment process – The organisation may discuss their proposal for accreditation informally with an assessor to seek advice and guidance in relation to their application.

Submission of documentation – All documentation required to demonstrate compliance with the assessment standard is submitted to the accreditation body for assessment.

Site visit – A team of trained assessors visits the organisation to review all procedures, process, documentation and operations for which accreditation is being sought. This may involve inspecting work in progress, speaking with staff, reviewing documentation of previous work, etc.

Dealing with non-compliances – Any processes found to deviate from written procedures or from the requirements of the standard against which they are being assessed are highlighted. Non-compliances are documented and the organisation informed and provided with opportunities to rectify these within a specified time frame before accreditation can be awarded.

Resubmission of documentation relating to non-compliances – Non-compliances should be addressed and the paperwork resubmitted for final assessment.

Awarding of accreditation certificate – Final accreditation certificate awarded. Accreditation is an ongoing activity and accredited organisations regularly undergo surveillance visits and are re-assessed every 4 years.

6.6 Accreditation and Standards for Forensic Science Internationally

International standards against which organisations are assessed are agreed through the ISO (derived from the Greek *isos* meaning 'equal'). ISO has a membership of 162 countries across the globe and standards are designed by consensus from relevant experts drawn from the member states.

For forensic science, the most adopted standards for practice within laboratories and organisations involved in crime scene examinations are, respectively, ISO/IEC 17025:2005, General Requirements for the Competence of Testing and Calibration Laboratories, and ISO/IEC 17020:2012, General Criteria for the Operation of Various Types of Bodies Performing Inspection.

In the United States the overarching adopted accreditation standards are ISO/IEC 17025 and ISO/IEC 17020, and the development of specific standards for forensic science is being led by the National Institute of Standards and Technology (NIST) as part of their activities for the U.S. National Commission on Forensic Science. NIST established the Organization of Scientific Area Committees (OSAC) with the remit to support the development of standards across the broad range of evidence types and the OSACs remain in existence despite the decision taken in 2017 by the US Government to close down the National Commission on Forensic Science.

Across Europe, again, the same ISO standards have been adopted. The European Network of Forensic Science Institutes (ENFSI) is involved in the development of guidance and, in some cases, standards for forensic science practice harmonised across the European continent through the activities of the 17 evidence-based working groups of ENFSI. Forensic science–related standards are passed through the European Committee for Standardization (CEN) and gain the prefix EN.

In Australia the accrediting body is the National Association of Testing Authorities (NATA) of Australia, which accredits forensic science providers against the relevant ISO standards that they have adopted. Accreditation can also include compliance with the Forensic Operations Module (Policy Circular 40, NATA, September 2012) available only to ISO accredited facilities.

6.7 Accreditation and Forensic Science in the UK

Accreditation to ISO standards in the UK is undertaken normally by the United Kingdom Accreditation Service (UKAS) which is the only national accreditation service in the UK.

UKAS accredits organisations against ISO/IEC 17020 and ISO/IEC 17025. Both standards are not bespoke to forensic science processes and, as such, there have been challenges in their implementation within the industry. They do, however, provide a framework against which validation of processes can be undertaken, including documentation of results, analysis, calibrations and procedures.

The ISO standards also include the necessary requirements for the inclusion of a quality management system detailing procedures (including auditing procedures) relating to the overall control of documents, and key roles and responsibilities of personnel.

The more technical aspects of the laboratory or crime scene process are usually detailed across a series of standard operating procedures which detail the equipment required, procedures for the relevant analytical process, validation methods, and so on. Both standards (ISO/IEC 17020 and ISO/ISE 17025) also provide for report writing and delivery of the final outputs as illustrated by the table of contents of ISO/IEC 17025 in Table 6.1.

Importantly, such standards also require the assessment of measurement uncertainty, a concept which has become increasingly important within forensic processes, although it can be one to which there has been a traditional resistance within various forensic science disciplines, particularly across the comparative processes such as fingerprint comparison, tool mark comparisons or ballistics comparisons, although attitudes are slowly changing in this regard.

Table 6.1 Table of Contents for ISO/IEC 17025

1 Scope
2 Normative references
3 Terms and definitions
4 Management requirements
- 4.1 Organization
- 4.2 Management system
- 4.3 Document control
- 4.4 Review of requests, tenders and contracts
- 4.5 Subcontracting of tests and calibrations
- 4.6 Purchasing services and supplies
- 4.7 Service to the customer
- 4.8 Complaints
- 4.9 Control of nonconforming testing and/or calibration work
- 4.10 Improvement
- 4.11 Corrective action
- 4.12 Preventive action
- 4.13 Control of records
- 4.14 Internal audits
- 4.15 Management reviews

5 Technical requirements
- 5.1 General
- 5.2 Personnel
- 5.3 Accommodation and environmental conditions
- 5.4 Test and calibration methods and method validation
- 5.5 Equipment
- 5.6 Measurement traceability
- 5.7 Sampling
- 5.8 Handling of test and calibration items
- 5.9 Assuring the quality of test and calibration results
- 5.10 Reporting the results

For crime scene examinations in the UK, the relevant accreditation standard against which organisations are measured is ISO/IEC 17020, and many international associations are now also recommending this as the appropriate standard. In 2015, UKAS produced RG 201 in order to provide specific guidance for the application of ISO/IEC 17020 to providers of crime scene examination services and forensic science providers, and some police forces within the UK are beginning to accredit against this standard.

In its provision of accreditation for forensic science UKAS also uses ILAC G19 as an accreditation guidance document which provides additional requirements specifically for forensic science provision (Table 6.2).

Accreditation of smaller specialist units operating, for example, as small businesses or within academic institutions is more challenging. The expense incurred for an accreditation process to be undertaken is often prohibitive where the organisation's core business is not the provision of forensic services (for example, in universities). In many cases such practitioners are engaged by the prosecuting authorities on a case-by-case basis.

In these situations the competence, specialist certification (if available) or authorisation of individuals is paramount, as is compliance with legal and discipline-specific requirements such as codes of practice in order for the individuals to act as expert witnesses. Indeed in April 2017 the Criminal Procedure Rules (2015) Rule 19 were modified to include a requirement for experts to follow a discipline specific Code of Practice should one exist.

Table 6.2 Table of Contents for ILAC G19

1 Scope
2 Terms and definitions
3 General guidance common to all activity modules in the forensic science process
4 Activity modules in the forensic science process
  4.1 Initial discussion regarding scene of crime attendance
  4.2 Undertaking initial actions at the scene of crime
  4.3 Developing a scene of crime investigation strategy
  4.4 Undertake scene of crime investigation
  4.5 Assess scene of crime findings and consider further examination
  4.6 Interpret and report findings from the scene of crime
  4.7 Examination and testing
  4.8 Interpretation of the results of examinations and tests
  4.9 Report from examinations and tests including interpretation of results
Annex A: Examples of disciplines undertaken by forensic units
Annex B: Bibliography
Annex C: Correlation chart

6.8 Role of the UK Forensic Science Regulator in UK Accreditation of Forensic Science Providers

Within the UK forensic science domain, the drive towards accreditation of organisations has been significant particularly since the introduction of the post of Forensic Science Regulator (FSR) in 2007. The Forensic Science Regulator's position arose as a suggestion as part of the UK government's response to a House of Commons Science and Technology Select Committee investigation 'forensic science on trial' (2005).

The Forensic Science Regulator is an independent public appointee sponsored by the UK home office and whose responsibilities include:

1. The identification of areas of forensic science practice where standards are required
2. The development of standards
3. The provision of advice in relation to compliance with standards
4. The investigation of non-compliance with standards or general poor practice within forensic science provision

Since its inception, the office of the Forensic Science Regulator has developed an overarching codes of practice document (Codes of Practice and Conduct for Forensic Science Providers and Practitioners in the Criminal Justice System, 2015), which sets out the required scientific quality standards for a range of forensic science disciplines together with a timetable by which these need to be implemented by forensic science providers within the domain of England and Wales. The codes are adopted by Northern Ireland and Scotland, although these regions are not within the regulator's formal jurisdiction.

The FSR has also published a series of guidance documents covering a range of evidence types demonstrating the necessary requirements for compliance against the Codes of Practice and Conduct.

Some specialist practitioner groups have also developed their own codes of practice documents generally through their professional bodies both in association with the Forensic Science Regulators office and independently, and these include pathology, archaeology, anthropology, fire investigation and podiatry.

6.9 Certification of Individual Practitioners

Certification of individual forensic practitioners continues to be a global challenge. In some circumstances this is assumed under accreditation processes, in that part of compliance with accreditation is a systematic testing of the competence of the employees who work within the accredited organisation. This can involve regular proficiency tests, declared and undeclared trials, and so on.

For some disciplines there are various certification programmes offered by their professional bodies. These can include formal examinations, casework review or a combination of both. The professional body normally requires recertification after a number of years, which can include a demonstration of continued practice, continuous professional development or re-examination. In Scotland forensic practitioners can also be authorised for the provision of analysis and reports relating to routine evidence under the Criminal Procedure (Scotland) Act 1995.

Of course certification in of itself does not necessarily imply competence to practice, and this separation continues to raise challenges across the sector.

6.10 Summary

Accreditation of forensic science providers is a necessary process in order to provide the courts with the confidence that organisations are undertaking work to recognised internationally accepted standards. The accreditation process is challenging within the forensic science domain, but a slow compliance across the purveyors of both scientific laboratory services and crime scene examination is in evidence in the UK and internationally.

How accreditation of smaller organisations and academic units who engage in casework at the request of the prosecution or defence teams is achieved is yet to be significantly debated and remains to be resolved in a sensible way so that such valuable services remain available to our justice systems.

Equally important is the certification of individual practitioners. This has been largely left to the professional bodies to define and tackle. Competence and fitness to practice are even more intangible. What is certain is that our judicial system requires competent and appropriately certified or authorised individuals working to a defined code of practice.

References

Association of Chief Police Officers in Scotland (2010). Disclosure in Criminal Proceedings. Manual of Guidance. https://www.btp.police.uk/pdf/ACPOS-Disclosure-in-Criminal-Proceedings-manual.pdf. Last accessed 17.01.2016.

British Medical Association (2007). British Medical Association Expert Witness Guidance. Downloaded http://bma.org.uk/-/media/Files/PDFs/Practical%20advice%20at%20work/Fees/expert%20witness%20guidance.pdf. Last accessed 17.01.2016.

Council of Europe (2010). European Convention on Human Rights. http://www.echr.coe.int/Documents/Convention_ENG.pdf. Last accessed 17.01.2016.

Criminal Procedure (Scotland) Act (1995). Chapter 46. Parts 280–284, pp528–534. http://www.legislation.gov.uk/ukpga/1995/46/contents. Last accessed 17.01.2016.

The Criminal Procedure Rules (2005). No. 384 (L.4). The Stationery Office. http://www.legislation.gov.uk/uksi/2005/384/pdfs/uksi_20050384_en.pdf. Last accessed 17.01.2016.

The Criminal Procedure Rules (2014). No. 1610 (L.26). The Stationery Office. http://www.legislation.gov.uk/uksi/2014/1610/contents/made. Last accessed 17.01.2016.

The Criminal Procedure Rules (2015). No. 1490 (L.18). The Stationery Office. http://www.legislation.gov.uk/uksi/2015/1490/contents/made. Last accessed 17.01.2016.

Crown Office and Procurator Fiscal Service (2015). Guidance Booklet for Expert Witnesses. The Role of the Expert Witness and Disclosure. http://www.copfs.gov.uk/images/Documents/Prosecution_Policy_Guidance/Guidelines_and_Policy/Guidance%20booklet%20for%20expert%20witnesses%20%20June%2015.pdf. Last accessed 17.01.2016.

Crown Prosecution Service (2010). Guidance Booklet for Experts Disclosure: Experts' Evidence, Case Management and Unused Material. http://www.cps.gov.uk/legal/d_to_g/disclosure_manual/annex_k_disclosure_manual/. Last accessed 17.01.2016.

Crown Prosecution Service (2014). Guidance on Expert Evidence. http://www.cps.gov.uk/legal/assets/uploads/files/expert_evidence_first_edition_2014.pdf. Last accessed 17.01.2016.

Edwards, R. (1969). *Freedom, Responsibility and Obligation*. Springer, London.

Forensic Science on Trial, Report of the House of Commons Select Committee on Science and Technology (2005). http://www.publications.parliament.uk/pa/cm200405/cmselect/cmsctech/96/96i.pdf. Last accessed 19.06.2016.

Forensic Science Regulator (2015). Legal Obligations. FSR-1-400, Issue 3. https://www.gov.uk/government/uploads/system/uploads/attachment_data/file/397694/FSR_Legal_Obligations_-_Issue_3.pdf. Last accessed 17.01.2016.

Forensic Science Regulator Annual Report, November 2014–2015, Dr Gillian Tully (2015). https://www.gov.uk/government/uploads/system/uploads/attachment_data/file/482248/2015_FSR_Annual_Report_v1_0_final.pdf. Last accessed 19.06.2016.

The Forensic Science Regulator, Codes of Practice and Conduct for Forensic Science Providers and Practitioners in the Criminal Justice System. Issue 3, February 2016. https://www.gov.uk/government/collections/forensic-science-providers-codes-of-practice-and-conduct. Last accessed 19.06.2016.

Haji, I. (2016). *Luck's Mischief: Obligation and Blameworthiness on a Thread*. Oxford University Press, Oxford.

ILAC G19:08:2014. http://ilac.org/news/ilac-g19082014-published/. Last accessed 19.06.2016.

ISO/IEC 17025:2005: General Requirements for the Competence of Testing and Calibration Laboratories. http://www.iso.org/iso/catalogue_detail.htm?csnumber=39883. Last accessed 19.06.2016.

ISO/IEC 17020:2012: General Criteria for the Operation of Various Types of Bodies Performing Inspection. http://www.iso.org/iso/catalogue_detail?csnumber=52994. Last accessed 19.06.2016.

Organisation for Scientific Area Committees (OSAC). http://www.nist.gov/forensics/osac/. Last accessed 19.06.2016.

Police and Criminal Evidence Act (1984). http://www.legislation.gov.uk/ukpga/1984/60. Last accessed 17.01.2016.

Policy Circular 40, NATA (September 2012). http://www.nata.com.au/nata/phocadownload/publications/Accreditation_criteria/Policy-Technical-Circulars/PolicyCircular40.pdf. Last accessed 19.06.2016.

R v Cooper (1998) EWCA Crim 2258.

UKAS-RG 201:2015: Accreditation of Bodies Carrying Out Scene of Crime Examination https://www.ukas.com/download/publications/RG%20201.pdf. Last accessed 19.06.2016.

Emerging Science in Court

7

FIONA RAITT

Contents

7.1 Introduction

Most of the book's contributors have emphasised the importance of ensuring the reliability of the expert evidence admitted to the courtroom. This chapter considers some specific issues of reliability that may arise when the scientific theory or the scientific technique cited as evidence is not yet established but is, instead, emerging science. Such science is sometimes referred to as novel science or science in its infancy. The admissibility of emerging science into the courtroom may be restricted or denied unless it can demonstrate that its credentials are trustworthy. In practice, this means that the presiding judge must be satisfied that the proposed expert evidence is reliable. In order to be assured of its admissibility, the underpinning science must have achieved the much sought-after status of 'general acceptance' within its relevant scientific community.[1] In particular, if the emerging science is to play a meaningful role in the courtroom, it must satisfy the criteria for reliability associated with the specific area of science to which it seeks to be aligned.

All common law jurisdictions have adopted some form of the test known as general acceptance. However, the pathway from discovery of new science and new scientific techniques to the stage where they are generally accepted within the relevant scientific community is fraught with hurdles. These must be overcome if the science is to be admissible in court and is to avoid being rejected as 'junk science' and therefore inadmissible (Huber 1993; Suni 2004).[2] Science that has not been established long enough to have had its reliability tested and its conclusions replicated on sufficient occasions is unlikely to command the wider support of its science community and will be denied the status of general acceptance.

By its very nature, the scientific method of validating new research findings and innovative techniques – for example, the rigorous testing in laboratory and other experimental settings – is a protracted process. Potentially, it may be many years before the process is completed, but that is unavoidable until the emerging science is considered safe to be introduced as new knowledge in criminal court proceedings.

7.2 Emerging Science and Avoiding Miscarriages of Justice

The risk of a miscarriage of justice arising from placing premature trust in emerging science is at the core of the precautionary principle, and a risk assessment could help with the delicate and finely balanced decisions that require to be taken (Foster et al. 2000). There are too many examples of previous failures in the justice system due to compliancy with established science or misguided excitement over the applications of new scientific findings (Jones 1994).[3]

If we applied the approach of the precautionary principle to the context of a criminal prosecution, we would obviously aim to avoid introducing science prematurely. But recognising when the application of the science is premature may ultimately be a very complex challenge for professional judgement. While we can design the procedures necessary to minimise the risks attached to emerging science, we cannot guarantee more than that. Science without risk is an oxymoron.

All this suggests that the effective regulation of emerging scientific evidence requires constant vigilance and is, in consequence, a major preoccupation for courts in the common law jurisdictions. A substantial body of case law and academic scholarship is devoted to the pursuit of a robust framework for admissibility of scientific evidence (for more extensive coverage see Roberts and Zuckerman 2010: 467).

7.3 The Pursuit of Reliable and Admissible Science

The admissibility standards that have been developed over the years within the common law countries have largely been driven by a series of Supreme Court decisions in the United States. The current rules for admissibility stretch back to the early landmark case of *Frye v United States* (1923) 293 F 1013,[4] a case that established some fundamental rules that are still pertinent today. Frye established the concept of general acceptance as a prerequisite for admissibility in court. This standard remains valid today, having been endorsed by the Supreme Court in the leading case of *Daubert v Merrell Dow Pharmaceuticals* (1993) 509 U.S. 579.[5]

Daubert amounted to a major reappraisal of the *Frye* test and resulted in a new set of guidelines from the Supreme Court governing the admissibility of scientific evidence (including one guideline that replicated general acceptance).

The court recommended that the trial judge take account of the following considerations when assessing the admissibility of the scientific evidence presented to the court:

1. Is the theory or technique at issue testable, or has it been tested?
2. Has the theory or technique been subjected to peer review and publication?
3. In the case of a particular technique, what is the known potential rate of error?
4. And finally, what is the degree of general acceptance in the scientific community of the theory or technique of these criteria?[6]

These considerations or guidelines are intended to act as preliminary tests of the quality and reliability of the science. One of the most important contributions from Supreme Court decisions to the terms of the process and standards for admissibility of expert evidence has been the insistence that the judiciary must take responsibility for the quality of the scientific evidence admitted. This compels judges to take on the role of gatekeeper. The trial judge is expected to identify and exclude scientific theories and techniques that cannot satisfy the preliminary test of reliability. The notion of judge as gatekeeper has its critics, including from among the judiciary as it is acknowledged, for example, that not all judges have received adequate training to negotiate concepts such as 'rates of error' or what might constitute 'satisfactory testing under actual field conditions'. Nonetheless, this role as gatekeeper was affirmed by the Supreme Court in the case of *Kumho Tire Co. v Carmichael* (1999) 526 U.S. 137[7] as intending to 'assign to the trial judge the task of ensuring that an expert's testimony both rests on a reliable foundation and is relevant to the task at hand'.[8] The common law countries have largely adopted these criteria or close versions of them in order to enable compatibility with their own legal systems. Most accept the principle of the judge as gatekeeper.

In common with most jurisdictions, the rules in the UK jurisdictions do not prescribe any specific limit to the number of experts a litigant can cite to appear in court as a witness. However, contributions are confined to suitably qualified experts, and judges encourage lawyers to expedite the court process by negotiating in advance of trial any evidence that is uncontested. In terms of controls on the quality of expertise in court, anyone appearing in an expert role is expected to meet some basic criteria. An expert is a witness whose area of knowledge is considered by the presiding judge to be 'beyond the understanding of the average juror'.[9] This is a relatively fluid and therefore imprecise test. It is unclear how to identify in advance of a trial which areas of knowledge will satisfy the test of being beyond the scope of jurors' competence. The concept certainly embraces an infinite scientific canvas that covers the disciplines of medicine and forensic science as well as engineering, anthropology and nuclear physics – and potentially no discipline is exempt.

The judicial logic underpinning this test is to ensure that the traditional judicial process should not simply be replaced by a system of trial by experts, given that 'the parties have invoked the decision of a judicial tribunal, and not an oracular pronouncement by an expert'.[10] Medical science and forensic technologies are constantly forging ahead, producing new complexities and unveiling fresh interpretations of the available science. There is therefore a constant tension between the desire of parties to take advantage of any fresh expert testimony favourable to their cause, and the pressure on the courts to control the admissibility of scientific evidence with little or no track record of reliability.

It might be assumed that emerging science should be treated with particular caution until it is sufficiently robust under cross-examination conditions and has demonstrable support from well-regarded members of the relevant scientific communities. However, the history of error concerning the use of emerging scientific theory or technique suggests the need for unfailing attention to detail and a healthy scepticism regardless of its age. This requirement was been echoed in the report produced by the National Research Council called 'Strengthening Forensic Science in the United States' (2009). This report examined a number of forensic science types including tool mark and firearms identification, DNA evidence, ridge pattern evidence, hair evidence, fibre evidence and bloodstain pattern analysis to name a few. The conclusion reached was that all of these evidence types had issues associated with them which resulted directly from a lack of robust scientific research underpinning each evidence type. The only exception to this was DNA evidence for which the background was based on sound scientific testing and research.

Although the length of time a theory or technique has been in the public domain is not necessarily a guarantee of its accuracy or reliability, the more exposure the science has had to scrutiny from peers and to cross-examination in the court process, the more likely it is that flaws or weaknesses will have been uncovered. Generally, well-established types of evidence, such as analyses of blood or fingerprints, are regularly presented by the parties to the court as 'agreed evidence' and are thus not challenged in court. There are always exceptions to this general rule of course, and a startling example was the upheaval caused in Scotland in 2011 with the publication of the Fingerprint Inquiry conducted by the Senior Northern Ireland Judge Sir Anthony Campbell, on behalf of the Scottish government.[11]

For present purposes, one of the key findings of the Fingerprint Inquiry was the startling revelation that the standard procedures adopted by the Scottish Fingerprint Service contained serious weaknesses. Specifically, the treatment of fingerprint evidence as fact, rather than opinion, was erroneous, a problem that was exacerbated where the comparison involved complex marks. As a result, Sir Anthony found that 'fingerprint examiners are presently ill-equipped to reason their conclusions as they are accustomed to regarding their conclusions as a matter of certainty and seldom challenged'.[12] This prevailing assumption that a fingerprint was conclusive evidence, dispensing with the need for any other kind of corroborating evidence, was entirely misplaced. The inquiry's outcome was particularly ironic for Scotland, a jurisdiction which is unique in the world in having as one of its baseline principles of criminal law the requirement that all admissible evidence must be corroborated.

The impact of the findings was immediate and profound. Scotland woke up to discover that over many decades, the prevailing philosophy of fingerprint examination in Scottish law had been seriously flawed. Its working principle treated fingerprint analysis as a matter of establishing a fact, whereas as the inquiry made clear it was, and could only ever be, capable of establishing an opinion. It was a conclusion that had far-reaching consequences. The Scottish justice system, virtually overnight, had to reconstruct itself, with many convictions revisited to ensure their validity. Fortunately, upheaval on such a scale is uncommon, but it is a powerful reminder of the dangers of complacency concerning the legitimacy of long-established practices and assumptions.

7.4 Challenging Evidence

Compared to the introduction of established science, when the evidence advanced in court is based on emerging science it presents far greater potential for adversarial challenge. Emerging science draws attention to the fact that knowledge is not fixed and static, but is subject to continual development, reappraisal and revision. Uncertainty is inherent in the scientific endeavour (Palmer and Hardaker 2011). And from a lawyer's perspective, the passage of time increases the potential for exposing the possibility of historical error in the interpretation of the science in previous convictions. There is therefore an opportunity, perhaps even duty, to challenge hitherto settled findings and understandings. After all, the emergence of new science, whether theoretical or technical, may give fresh hope to those prisoners who maintain their innocence as well as to victims of unsolved crimes and those still seeking explanations of past events.[13]

The increasing influence of science in the courtroom poses a significant challenge to lay juries in the adversarial process. Generally, the courts are mindful of the scope for scientific evidence to influence unduly the deliberations of jurors. The concern is that jurors might attach too much significance to the opinions of expert witnesses, simply because of their expert status, instead of focusing on the facts led in evidence from other non-expert witnesses.

Recent jury research has described how jurors may be challenged in their understanding of complex evidence. Even unfamiliarity with court practices can be disorientating at a time when jurors are expected to concentrate fully as the trial unfolds (Thomas 2010). There is no reason to assume that members of the judiciary, legal profession or a panel of jurors will have any particular qualifications in scientific knowledge, let alone any training or advanced education in the scientific method. On the contrary, poor educational levels in science and mathematics across the UK population are a national concern, and not confined to a particular social group (Royal Society 2007). It is reasonable to speculate that when scientific evidence presented in court is in its early development, it may pose an additional challenge for the trier of fact due to its as yet imprecise status. Therefore, both the judge and the trier of fact rely heavily on expert testimony being lucid, accurate and current. When experts fail in any of these respects, a miscarriage of justice is more likely. An example of when poor communication by an expert created exactly this issue was the catastrophic misrepresentation of statistical evidence by Professor Sir Roy Meadow, a perceived expert in paediatrics who was woefully deficient in his understanding of statistics in the context of cot deaths. His misleading evidence contributed to a series of cases of wrongful convictions and imprisonment of several women (Royal College of Pathologists 2004).

The judicial response to the principle of admitting emerging science has been unequivocal in promoting its value provided certain parameters are followed. Some key guidance was set out in *R v Harris and Others* (2005),[14] where the English Court of Appeal ruled on four conjoined cases concerning the phenomenon then known as shaken baby syndrome (now known as non-accidental head injury [NAHI]). The court in *Harris* acknowledged the contingent state of science with respect to the uncertainties associated with the phenomenon, the precise cause of which is still thought to be extremely hard to determine and remains a site of deep medical division.

The court ruled on the conjoined appeals involving the deaths of several infants. Rather than ruling against admitting such evidence altogether until it was deemed safe science and thus reliable, the Court of Appeal urged a bolder but measured approach. Lord Justice Gage noted obiter, 'in our judgement, developments in scientific thinking should not be kept from the court, simply because they remain at the stage of a hypothesis'.[15] Obviously, it is of the first importance that the true status of the expert's evidence is frankly indicated to the court. Lord Gage's observations are an important reminder to experts that the duty of the expert is to the court and that the interests of justice are paramount.

When all the evidence has been led at a trial, it is the duty of the presiding judge to sum up the evidence and then charge the jury with their responsibilities in deliberating over the evidence and in reaching a verdict. Little research has been undertaken concerning juror comprehension of their duties or their capacity to comprehend judicial instructions as to how to carry out those duties. Studies in England by Cheryl Thomas (2010) are the most recent, and her results concluded that 'while over half of the jurors at Winchester (68%) perceived the judge's directions as easy to understand, only a minority fully understood the directions in terms used by the judge'.

When the science in question concerns emerging science that has not yet established its status, it can prompt the trial judge, or subsequently an appellate judge, to clarify the parameters of the application of that science and the role of the expert. The instinctive judicial caution is neatly captured in the often-cited warning from Lord Justice Lawton in *R v Turner*: 'If on the proven facts a judge or jury can form their own conclusions without help, then the opinion of an expert is unnecessary. In such a case if it is given dressed up in scientific jargon it may make judgement more difficult'.[16] The *Turner* case concerned the potential for behavioural science findings to mislead the jury, an area of knowledge, which the court felt, ought to be within that of the average member of the public. The case has been much criticised in academic circles. The sentiment behind the Lawton dictum would likely carry much less purchase in the context of emerging science.

7.5 Reforms

In 2011 the Law Commission for England and Wales published its report on expert evidence in the criminal courts (The Law Commission of England and Wales 2011). Within this the commission made extensive and detailed recommendations, drawing heavily on reforms that had been introduced in other English-speaking jurisdictions. Its recommendations including the following issues for the trial judge when considering the reliability of expert opinion evidence:

1. the quality of the data on which the expert opinion is based and the validity of the methods used …
2. whether the opinion explains how safe or unsafe are any inferences from the data,
3. the extent to which any material upon which the expert's opinion is based has been reviewed & supported by others with relevant expertise, for example, peer reviewed,
4. the extent to which the expert's opinion is based on material falling outside the expert's own field of expertise

5. the completeness of the information available to the expert, and whether the expert took account of all relevant information in arriving at the opinion
6. whether there is a range of expert opinion on the matter in question; and, if there is, where in the range the expert's opinion lies within it
7. whether the expert's methods followed established practice in the field; and, if they did not, whether the reason for the divergence has been properly explained.

The Law Commission proposals include the following: 'We recommend that a trial judge who has to determine whether an expert's opinion evidence is sufficiently reliable to be admitted should be directed to have regard to [not exhaustive list]: the quality of the data on which the expert's opinion is based, and the validity of the methods used – what degree of precision or margin of uncertainty might affect the reliability of results'[17]. The report was warmly received by both practitioners and academics, inspiring numerous national projects aimed at taking forward the proposals. However, the government declined to legislate to make the report's recommendations binding, instead relying upon good practice evolving within the legal and scientific professions. A notable Scottish response was the Scottish Universities Insight Institute (SUII) programme 'Scots Law of Evidence in the Digital Age – Fit for Purpose?' which drew in an international set of collaborators (SUII 2011). The collaborators came from varying disciplines, including members of the judiciary, advocates, forensic scientists and academics.

The 2-day programme culminated in a report which concluded that Scotland's present rules do not provide a rigorous modern framework for the use and management of expert scientific evidence in court and despite the passage of time, the main recommendations remain valid. Given the increasing importance of science to society in general, and as a source of evidence within the courts in particular, the relationship between law and science deserves careful nurturing and regular review. Although some forensic science such as fingerprint and DNA evidence is well established, that does not mean that such evidence is invariably safe (SUII 2011). Moreover, scientific and technological developments are continually stretching the parameters of what it is possible to prove and with what degree of reliability. Novel or emerging scientific theories or techniques should be treated with caution. But while it is right to be wary of the reliability of science that is in its infancy, the English Court of Appeal has warned against rejecting it outright. For example, in regard to emerging science in cases of alleged 'shaken baby syndrome', Gage LJ observed in *R v Harris and Others* (2005) EWCA Crim. 1980 at 270: Developments in scientific thinking and techniques should not be kept from the court simply because they remain at the stage of a hypothesis.

The SUII (2011) report discusses the circumstances in which, provided sufficient care is taken, new scientific techniques can be (and have been) used effectively, including in Scotland, to secure convictions. What constitutes 'sufficient care' is the critical issue. As the report notes, 'The [English] Law Commission and the Forensic Regulator both support the introduction of novel science to the court providing it is not used inappropriately or outwith the boundaries of its capabilities. As novel research develops and embeds within the scientific community, protocols, procedures and standards need to be regularly updated and modified. The admissibility and degree of weight and reliance placed on the evidence must match the maturity of the emerging science' (SUII 2011).

The need to balance the twin interests of caution over the reliability of the science and the desire not to deprive the proof process of evidence that might incriminate or exonerate is at the heart of the SUII (2011) report's recommendation. The report recommended that Scotland should adopt the proposal set out in the English Law Commission's 2011 report 'Expert Evidence in Criminal Proceedings' for a new test of reliability. This test of reliability would determine the admissibility of scientific evidence in courts. The last systematic appraisal undertaken in Scotland of the relationship between law and science in the courtroom was more than 30 years ago. Recent High Court appeal cases, together with the publication in December 2011 of the Fingerprint Inquiry into the issues arising in the Shirley McKie case, remind us of some of the difficulties that expert scientific evidence poses for the justice system, suggesting a review is overdue.

7.6 The Gatekeeping Role of the Judge

While it is up to the trier of fact to assess the reliability of the evidence they hear, most jurisdictions have moved to a more directive role for the judge. Regardless of the complexity or density of the testimony, the trial judge cannot derogate from their responsibility to guide juries through the evidence that has been given in court while being even-handed with both parties.

Recent judgements from the Scottish courts highlight two issues that affect emerging science. First is the vortex created when there is significant dispute within the expert opinions offered, as this raises the scope for confusion among the jurors. For example, in the case of *Walker v HM Advocate*, evidence to the court was provided by 15 separate experts, representing seven different fields of expertise, namely haematology, radiology, paediatric respiratory medicine, endocrinology, pathology, statistics and microbiology.[18] There was no consensus among the experts on the cause of the death. However, one can imagine that, in such circumstances, novel or emerging science might appear riskier to jurors who have to decide which expert view was the most reliable. In this case, after all the evidence had been presented, neither the prosecutor nor the defence counsel opted to follow the normal procedure and address the jury on how to interpret the expertise they had heard. This unusual decision was apparently made on the basis that the evidence was so complicated there was a risk that they, the lawyers, would 'get it wrong'.[19] The defence counsel colourfully described the quantity of expert evidence as 'a mountain, maybe a swamp of professional opinion to assess'.[20] Although the trial judge directed the jury on how to approach the assessment of expert evidence, he declined to 'rehearse the evidence'.[21] The Appeal Court acknowledged that trial judges have considerable discretion in the manner in which they give juries directions. However, the court was unanimous in considering that the judge must provide *some* guidance as it was essential for juries to have the tools to enable them to reach a decision through a reasoned process. It is notable that Article 6 of the European Court of Human Rights (ECHR) requires a fair trial to be one arrived at through a reasoned verdict.[22]

This is particularly important where, as in *Walker v HM Advocate* (2011) HCJAC,[23] the medical science was disputed, and the cause of death could not even be ascertained. The Appeal Court held that the trial judge's failure to address the position of each of the principal experts amounted to a material misdirection to the jury and the conviction was quashed.

Another type of complexity for fact-finders arises when the expert evidence is emerging and is so distinctive that it is not within the experience of the trial judge, as this increases the risk of an inadequate charge to the jury. This issue occurred in the case of Kimberley Hainey in 2013[24] where the judges both at the trial level and on appeal failed to appreciate the distinctive nature of the scientific discipline involved – forensic anthropology. As a result, the evidence of two of the experts appeared to be treated as if their discipline was indistinguishable from mainstream medical science, a position that was misleading and unhelpful for the jury. Neither counsel nor the trial judge understood the significance of this or of its potential to mislead the fact-finder.

7.7 Conclusion

In any given case, the parties will likely contest both the facts and the expert's interpretation of them. Generally, the more established the science, the more difficult it will be to mount an effective challenge. The UK courts limit the contribution of experts to those areas of knowledge beyond the understanding of the average juror. There is some anxiety to ensure the traditional judicial process should not simply be replaced by a system of trial by experts. This is challenged as medical science and technology develop, producing new complexities and understandings. This creates a constant tension between the desire of parties to have expert testimony favourable to their cause admitted and the pressure on the courts to control the admissibility of science with no track record of reliability. Despite this tension with new techniques, the length of time a theory or technique has been in the public domain is not a guarantee of its accuracy or reliability. However, it can be argued that the greater the exposure science has had to scrutiny from peers and to cross-examination in the court process, the more likely it is that flaws or weakness will be uncovered. Thus, evidence of analyses of blood or fingerprints is regularly presented by the parties to the court as 'agreed'. At the opposite end of the scale, novel or emerging science offers far greater opportunities for dispute. The state of knowledge is not static. It is subject to continual experiment, reappraisal and revision. From a lawyer's perspective this inevitably increases the possibility of historical error and opportunity, indeed, perhaps duty, to challenge the status quo.

McCreight v HM Advocate (2009) HCJAC 69 concerned a referral to the Appeal Court after fresh evidence showed that an expert witness at a murder trial had overstated the figure for the concentration of chloroform in the liver by a factor of 1000. While at one level this was simply human error on a colossal scale, the lack of any systematic procedure for testing the evidential reliability or validity of an expert's calculations in such situations is problematic. At the very least, it does not encourage counsel to embark upon a focused examination of expert witnesses as to the derivation of their calculations, or indeed similar ones relating to statistical probabilities. As may be recalled, misinterpretation of statistical probabilities was central to the misleading evidence of Professor Sir Roy Meadow in the case against Sally Clarke.[25]

In *Walker v HM Advocate* (2011) HCJAC, the complexity of the competing accounts from 15 scientific experts of the likely cause of death of a baby in 1982 resulted in the trial judge declining to give the jury any directions on how to evaluate the evidence. Although the ground of appeal in Walker[26] was principally concerned with the judicial responsibility to give clear directions to the jury, the absence of any compulsion within the present Scottish adversarial system on parties to identify uncontroversial evidence and any common ground, or even to narrow down the contested issues, is fundamentally inefficient and unhelpful to fact-finders.

By its very nature expert scientific evidence in the courtroom, is complex and considerably beyond the general knowledge of the fact-finder. Common concerns across jurisdictions include the quality of the evidence given by some experts, the capability of lawyers in examining and cross-examining scientific experts, the parameters of judicial discretion in admitting or refusing to admit expert evidence, and whether juries are well placed to evaluate expert scientific evidence. Most countries have tackled these concerns by imposing a gatekeeping role on the trial judge to evaluate the reliability of the scientific evidence that is admitted in court.

Reliability should be a priority for the admissibility of all scientific evidence, but it arises more acutely when considering emerging science. The SUII (2011) report recommendations propose that Scotland addresses these concerns through improved better professional education at all levels, with the primary objective a robust reliability framework for admissibility of scientific evidence. These steps should be linked to the Codes of Practice developed by the UK Regulator[27] and the Practitioner Guides being published by the RSS.[28]

By its very nature expert scientific evidence in the courtroom is complex and considerably beyond the general knowledge of the fact-finder. Common concerns across jurisdictions include the quality of the evidence given by some experts, the capability of lawyers in examining and cross-examining scientific experts, the parameters of judicial discretion in admitting or refusing to admit expert evidence, and whether juries are well placed to evaluate expert scientific evidence. Most countries have tackled these concerns by imposing a gatekeeping role on the trial judge to evaluate the reliability of the scientific evidence that is admitted in court.

Notes

1. *Frye v United States* (1923) 293 F 1013.
2. 'Junk science' was a term first popularised by Huber, Peter. 1992. *Galileo's Revenge: Junk Science in the Courtroom*. New York: Basic Books; and Suni, Ellen Y. 2004. Science, Forensic Science, Junk Science and Expert Opinion Testimony. http://www1.law.umkc.edu/suni/wrongful_convictions/Junk%20Science.htm.
3. *R v Anne Maguire and Others* (1992) 94 Cr. App. R. 133 as summarised by Rosenberg, Joshua. 1992. Miscarriages of Justice. In *Criminal Justice Under Stress*, edited by E. Stockdale and S. Casale. Blackstone Press.
4. *Frye v United States* (1923) 293 F 1013.
5. *Daubert v Merrell Dow Pharmaceuticals, Inc.* (1993) 509 U.S. 579, 589–592.
6. *Daubert v Merrell Dow Pharmaceuticals, Inc.* (1993) 509 U.S. 579, 589–592.
7. *Kumho Tire Co. v Carmichael* (1999) 526 U.S. 137.
8. The appeal judges were affirming this role as laid out in the Federal Rules of Evidence 702, *Kumho Tire Co. v Carmichael* (1999) 526 U.S. 137, p. 141.
9. *R v Turner* (1975) Q.B. 834, 841.
10. *Davie v Mags of Edinburgh* (1953) S.C. 1934.
11. The Fingerprint Inquiry. 2011. The Fingerprint Inquiry Report. The Fingerprint Inquiry Scotland. http://www.webarchive.org.uk/wayback/archive/20150428160106/http://www.thefingerprintinquiryscotland.org.uk/inquiry/files/TheFingerprintInquiryReport_High_res.pdf.
12. Page 739 of the Fingerprint Inquiry. 2011. The Fingerprint Inquiry Report. The Fingerprint Inquiry Scotland. http://www.webarchive.org.uk/wayback/archive/20150428160106/http://www.thefingerprintinquiryscotland.org.uk/inquiry/files/TheFingerprintInquiryReport_High_res.pdf.
13. Innocence Project. http://www.innocenceproject.org.

14. *R v Harris and Others* (2005) EWCA Crim. 1980.
15. *R v Harris and Others* (2005) EWCA Crim. 1980 at 270.
16. *R v Turner* (1975) Q.B. 834, 841.
17. See para. 3.62, p. 19 of the Law Commission Paper No. 325. 2011. *Expert Evidence in Criminal Proceedings in England and Wales.*
18. *Walker v HM Advocate* (2011) HCJAC.
19. *Walker v HM Advocate* (2011) HCJAC para. 32.
20. *Walker v HM Advocate* (2011) HCJAC para. 32.
21. *Walker v HM Advocate* (2011) HCJAC para. 34.
22. *Taxquet v Belgium* (926/05) (2012) 54 E.H.R.R. 26; (2011) Crim. L.R. 236.
23. *Walker v HM Advocate* (2011) HCJAC.
24. *Hainey v HM Advocate* (2013) HCJAC 47.
25. *R v Clark* (2000) EWCA Crim. 54.
26. *Walker v HM Advocate* (2011) HCJAC.
27. See https://www.gov.uk/government/organisations/forensic-science-regulator.
28. See http://www.rss.org.uk/RSS/Influencing_Change/Statistics_and_the_law/Practitioner_guides/RSS/Influencing_Change/Current_projects_sub/Statistics_and_the_law_sub/Practitioner_guides.aspx?hkey=2cfdf562-361e-432e-851b-ef6ff5254145.

References

European Court of Human Rights. http://www.echr.coe.int/Documents/Convention_ENG.pdf [accessed 21 August 2016].

Foster, Kenneth R., Paolo Vecchia, and Michael H. Repacholi. 2000. Science and the Precautionary Principle. *Science* 288(5468): 979–981.

Huber, Peter W. 1993. *Galileo's Revenge: Junk Science in the Courtroom.* New York, NY: Basic Books.

Jones, Carol A. G. 1994. *Expert Witnesses: Science, Medicine and the Practice of Law.* Oxford: Oxford University Press.

Law Commission Paper No. 325. 2011. *Expert Evidence in Criminal Proceedings in England and Wales.*

Mangrum, Richard Collin. 1999. Kuhmo Tire Company: The Expansion of the Court's Role in Screening Every Aspect of Every Expert's Testimony at Every Stage of the Proceedings. *Creighton Law Review* 33: 525.

Palmer, Timothy Noel, and Paul James Hardaker. 2011. Handling Uncertainty in Science. *Philosophical Transactions of the Royal Society of London A: Mathematical, Physical and Engineering Sciences* 369(1956): 4681–4684.

Roberts, Paul. 1994. Science in the Criminal Process. *Oxford Journal of Legal Studies* 14(4): 469–506.

The Royal College of Pathologists and the Royal College of Paediatrics and Child Health. 2004. *Sudden Unexpected Death in Infancy: A Multi-Agency Protocol for Care and Investigation.* http://www.rcpch.ac.uk/sites/default/files/page/SUDI_report_for_web.pdf [accessed 13 January 2019].

Royal Society. A 'State of the Nation' Report. *Science and Mathematics Education, 14–19.* https://royalsociety.org/~/media/Royal_Society_Content/education/policy/state-of-nation/SNR2-full-report.pdf [accessed 13 January 2019].

SUII. 2011. *Scots Law of Evidence in the Digital Age – Fit for Purpose?* http://www.scottishinsight.ac.uk/Portals/50/ScotsLawEvidence.pdf.

Suni, Ellen Y. 2004. Science, Forensic Science, Junk Science and Expert Opinion Testimony. http://www1.law.umkc.edu/suni/wrongful_convictions/Junk%20Science.htm [accessed 27 July 2016].

Thomas, Cheryl. 2010. *Are Juries Fair?* London: Ministry of Justice.

Zuckerman, Adrian A. S., and Paul Roberts. 1989. *The Principles of Criminal Evidence.* Oxford: Clarendon Press.

Statistics and the Expert Witness

8

DAVID LUCY AND
LUCINA HACKMAN

Contents

This chapter considers the use of statistics within forensic science, especially its relevance to the interpretation of evidence, and presentation of that interpretation to the court of law. Forensic science refers to those elements of the physical sciences which are used to support law in the investigation of crimes, or suspected crimes, and to analyse the evidence which accrues during an investigation for presentation in a court of law. As a court of law is the end result of this involvement, and most members of a court are not scientists, the techniques and methods used by forensic scientists have to be guaranteed by the forensic science community to be not only as scientifically robust as possible, but also legally relevant.

An important aspect of distinguishing truth from falsehood in both the physical and the social sciences is the way in which the respective merits, or demerits, of any proposition or idea are open to some form of scrutiny. For most sciences this takes the form of peer review and debate in the scientific press. When those sciences are utilised in the courtroom, however, this peer review process is sometimes considered to be partially replaced by the court process of evaluation of the evidence. This evaluation is undertaken by members of the judiciary as they determine the admissibility of the evidence, and once admitted before a jury it is again tested in open court, which is, unless special circumstances prevail, open to those with any interest in the matter being decided. Many argue that in the adversarial system this judicial scrutiny is sufficient to ensure that only robust science, which is underpinned by the highest-quality research, is presented in court, and that any science of poor or inadequate quality would quickly be exposed. However, a look at the cases considered by the Appeal Court of England and Wales demonstrates that this is not always the case (Henderson 2002). The Law Commission report (2011) examined the role of the judge, court and adversarial system in relation to this presentation of evidence and used this as a basis to make recommendations for the gatekeeping role of the judge in relation to admissibility of forensic evidence. It is interesting to note that while a number of issues have been identified in relation to the presentation of expert evidence, many of the miscarriages of justice that led to the formulation of the Law Commission report (2011) had at their core the use of statistics in a court by an expert witness.

The expert witness may interact with statistics at a number of points during their role in an investigation and will occasionally be asked to present and interpret statistics for the court. Many of the issues which are encountered within this process were summarised in the 'Strengthening Forensic Science in the United States' report (National Research Council 2009,) which underlined the fact that, unlike the development of other scientific methodologies, many forensic techniques were 'developed empirically within the forensic community, with little foundation on scientific theory or analysis'. While this report examined forensic science within the United States, its conclusions in relation to forensic evidence are relevant to forensic science in the UK. Many of the issues of the lack of scientific methodology and analysis highlighted within the report arose from the use of statistics in the courtroom (National Research Council 2009). Certainly, the lack of empirical research in relation to some evidence types has left the forensic scientist without a firm basis upon which to create some measure of uncertainty for their evidence (Christensen et al. 2014). This relates both to those sciences which can be considered to be more traditional and have a long history of use within the courtroom, such as fingerprint analysis or tool mark comparison, and to those that have been more recently brought to use in the forensic arena, such as gait analysis. It is unfortunate that there has been a tendency to accept that because an evidence type has been used for many years, and used to help to convict or exonerate, on many occasions, it must be therefore be robust and reliable (Kutcher 2001; Fingerprint Inquiry 2011; National Research Council 2009). Increasingly this has been shown to not be the case at all; indeed, quite the opposite is true. Of note is DNA evidence, which is one of the areas of forensic science which has a proven robust scientific background, and is perhaps where the fewest challenges have been linked to the analysis of evidence (Saks and Koehler 1991). Even DNA is not without issues, however, and those lie in both the presentation and interpretation of DNA analytical results in the courtroom.[1] Continued development may be the cause of greater statistical pitfalls of this science, as greater sensitivity in detection raises further questions of analysis in relation to commingled (mixed) DNA profiles. While tests can identify that commingled profiles are present, statistics has had to try and keep up with the requirement to successfully separate and interpret commingling for the court (Balding 2013). This has led to decisions by judges to rule DNA mixture evidence as inadmissible,[2] although an examination of the Court of Appeal's rulings demonstrates that this is not always the case.[3]

An expert witness presents evidence and opinion on a field in which they hold expertise through study and research, and that their expertise has to be beyond that which is expected of a member of the jury.[4] The statistical sciences play a pivotal role in the formation of that opinion since not all forensic evidence points unequivocally to a single conclusion. Instead, many conclusions may be possible, some more strongly supported by the evidence than others. Statistics is the science of resolving these uncertainties, and so any expert witness may be asked in examination or cross-examination to comment upon matters which are to a greater or lesser degree statistical. This is the case even if they are not themselves statisticians as there is an expectation that they will have an understanding that allows them to utilise statistics in order to interpret their own evidence types. Statistics will therefore have a critical role to play in both the analysis of evidence and the ways in which that evidence is presented in court.

This chapter looks at the areas in which the expert witness and statistics interact, and the responsibilities of the expert witness in relation to those interactions using examples from court cases to illustrate some issues which have been encountered. These reflect the need to reconcile the requirements of the court with the professional conduct of the expert witness who has been asked to give an assessment of evidence which may be inherently uncertain.

To give a sense of the scale and scope of the use of forensic evidence in court, the lord chief justice for England and Wales, the Right Honourable Lord Thomas of Cwngiedd (2014), noted that 'the vast majority of serious cases, and a significant proportion of all Crown Court cases, now include presentation of one or more types of forensic evidence'. The fact that many cases go on to be considered by the Court of Appeal based on the forensic science which was presented as part of the original case only highlights the fact that problems still arise with this type of evidence. The cases discussed here shed light on the types of error, mistakes and disagreements that can arise in the statistical science which are presented as evidence in the courts and have given rise to a great deal of discussion of ways in which these errors can be avoided.

Much forensic science still concentrates on individualisation. This is the process of 'matching' samples, usually in the form of evidence found at a scene, with a potential source (Champod 2000). The 'matching' of sample and source usually relies on identified characteristics and the comparison of these characteristics. One of the issues that has come to the fore in relation to this individualisation process is the poor research base that the interpretation of so-called matches are based upon (Saks and Koehler 2008). There has been limited research, databases and testing of error and reliability for the scientists to utilise as a base from which to development their statistics (National Research Council 2009; Saks and Koehler 2008). This has in the past led to a situation in which the scientist has based the probability of a match on their own and their colleagues' past experience (Koehler and Saks 2010; Saks and Koehler 2005). Quite correctly, this is no longer an acceptable approach and mathematical models are increasingly being created to demonstrate the likelihood of the evidential sample and the source having come from the same origins. Due to the lack of research and poor, or non-existent, databases with which to support the statistical analysis, evidence brought before a court using these mathematical models has, on occasion, fallen short.[5]

The issue of matching and the probabilities that are created from it have become a subject of debate within the literature where the idea of the existence of a definite match between evidential sample and source is interrogated (Kaye 2010; Koehler and Saks 2010; Page et al. 2011; Saks and Koehler 2005, 2008). There have been a number of attempts by forensic scientists to argue that characteristics, especially when in combination with other characteristics, can be considered unique; however, this has been shown to be based on faulty reasoning, and without statistical basis (Koehler and Saks 2010). Other arguments for uniqueness have been shown to be based on flawed research methodologies (Christensen 2004; Page et al. 2011). It is safe to say that forensic scientists will continue to be asked to undertake comparisons, but it is imperative for them to also use statistical methods in a balanced manner, supported by robust scientific research and sound probabilistic reasoning. This has in the past been an advantage for DNA whose origins were firmly based on the biological genetic population theory prior to its use as a tool in investigations; however, due to greater sensitivity of instrumentation the deconvolution of mixed-profile DNA samples remains a mathematical challenge,[6] albeit one that is being researched within the discipline (Balding 2003).

Once the interpretation of the evidence is complete, the presentation of this analysis in court is where issues with statistics comes to the fore as this is where the scientist's suppositions are fully tested and made public. Until this point, the expert will have worked as the provider of information to an investigation team. In court, their evidence will be scrutinised, initially by the judge as gatekeeper, who will assess admissibility, and then by the legal representatives of the Crown and defence, potentially by opposing experts and then finally by the jury themselves. This system is not without its faults and these were iterated and explored by the Law Commission report (2011). It is not only in relation to the admissibility of the evidence itself and the statistical evidence, but the potential for the stated evidence to be presented in such a way that it can be easily misinterpreted, falling into an error in logic known as the prosecutor's fallacy (Aitken and Taroni 2004). Given the number of instances of where this fallacy is encountered in some form or another, it is clear that this is an easy error to make when evaluating the types of evidence that an expert witness is often involved with interpreting. Put very simply, it is the act of presuming that the probability of a 'match' as iterated by the expert is equivalent to the probability of the innocence of the individual accused. So a statement given by an expert that the random match probability is 1 in a million equates to the chance of seeing a specific blood type if the blood came from someone other than the accused. With the prosecutor's fallacy this is interpreted as meaning that the chance that that the blood came from someone else is 1 in a million. So the jury, rather than asking themselves, 'What is the probability that the defendant is innocent given this evidence match?' are actually persuaded to ask themselves, 'What is the probability that the defendant matches the description given that he or she is innocent?' (Thomas and Schumann 1987).

Thomson and Schumann (1987) also suggest the existence of a defender's fallacy. In this the potential innocence of an individual is calculated by the fact that their match probabilities place them in a relatively large group. They use the example of an individual having a blood type which is only found in 1% of the population. 'In a city of 1 million there would be approximately 10,000 people with this blood type'. The suggestion would be that this would indicate little weight in the evidence as there is only a small possibility of this match indicating the presence of the accused (1 in 10,000 people).

The ability of the jury to understand the basic probabilities which are presented in court has been questioned by a number of authors; this is especially highlighted with the increase in the use of DNA evidence, which, while based on a sounder base scientifically, does present the court with statistical probabilities which they may not normally come across (Donnelly 2005; Koehler and Kaye 1991). The numbers that can be presented are often large and their significance may be difficult to put into context (Donnelly 2005). Tests on the understanding of undergraduates of statistical evidence presented in cases suggest that the relationship between presented statistics and the utilisation of this information in the decision-making process might not be linear (Nobles and Schiff 2005). It is difficult to know how the results of these studies extrapolate to the actual experience of the jury who may not have the advantage of a university education.

Despite a long history of the use of probability in relation to forensic evidence, issues still arise. The examples presented below are drawn from a selection of case law from the Court of Appeal of England and Wales. These cases place the issues discussed above into the framework of forensic casework and highlight the pitfalls, disagreements and issues that can await the expert witness during their role in a forensic investigation. For some cases, the issues were proven to be around the development of the strength of the match – that is, the probabilities surrounding the strength of the match. Others surround the presentation of statistics within the courtroom itself. The fact that these issues were discussed in the Court of Appeal underlines that they have merit and it is with these considerations in mind that any expert should work.

What is clear is that statistics can play a role in the misinterpretation of the importance of the evidence presented. This was brought to the fore in the now infamous presentation of statistics by Sir Roy Meadows during *R v Clark*.[7] Having presented the findings of research which had demonstrated that the chance of a single SIDS (sudden infant death syndrome) death in a family was 1 in 8543, Sir Roy Meadows was asked what the chances were of two cot deaths occurring in any one family. On the advice of a statistician, who assumed independence between the events, Sir Roy Meadows calculated that the probability for two such events would be 1 in 8543 multiplied by 1 in 8543, and therefore 1 in 73 million, a seemingly very rare case. This example raises a number of issues in relation to the statistical evidence. First, it underlines the fact that statistics should not be used naïvely. Here, the independence assumption was clearly incorrect. Little thought was given to conditioning factors, such as how an undiagnosed genetic condition would change the probabilities, which were not taken into account when undertaking this simplistic calculation (Dawid 2004). Second, and some would argue, probably the greatest issue with this evidence, was the potential way in which this sort of statistical evidence may be perceived by the jury during their decision making (Buchanan 2007). The way in which the probability was presented may have suggested that the innocent explanation for the facts was highly unlikely, suggesting that the opposite, or guilty explanation, is the correct one. This is a good example of the prosecutor's fallacy and in cases such as these, there is only one of two possibilities – either the accused did cause the death of the child or she did not. In this case, if the jury accepted that there was only a 1 in 73 million chance that the death of the child was due to natural causes, it would be hard to avoid taking the step to concluding that there was also the chance that there was a 1 in 73 million chance that the accused was not guilty (Nobles and Schiff 2005).

DNA evidence, while praised by the 2009 'Strengthening Forensic Science in the United States' report for having a sound statistical basis, has been shown to have issues in both the interpretation and the presentation of that interpretation in court. Many of the problems stem from mixed profiles and the calculations required to separate these and assign probabilities to those matches. In some cases, the scientists involved did not make an attempt to separate the profiles due to their complexity, and this has in itself caused further issues; however, the Appeal Court has also allowed cases in which a DNA mixture led to a lack of statistical interpretation.

The strength of a DNA match can and does come into focus when alternative possibilities are offered. In *R v Watters*,[8] for example, the probability of a DNA profile found at a burglary scene matching to the accused changed from 1 in 86 million for four of the scenes and 1 in 79,000 for the fifth if the accused did not have a close relative to 1 in 267 and 1 in 32, respectively, if the defendant had two brothers, which he did. This demonstrates how extra information can radically alter the strength of a match delivered by the expert.

Calculation of the strength of a match can cause disagreements between experts who otherwise agree on the presence of DNA profiles within a sample. In *R v Hookway*,[9] this was the central issue and accurately communicating the areas of disagreement and agreement to the jury was vitally important.

A number of issues have arisen in relation to the ability to calculate the strength of matches as a direct result of a lack of database upon which to develop accurate estimates for the probabilities involved. Ear prints,[10] gait analysis,[11] gunshot residue[12] and CCTV identification[13] have all been forensic evidence types which have given cause for cases to come to the Court of Appeal. All of these have proven weak when attempts at meaningful comparisons have been made due to the lack of databases and research which have underpinned the premises that have been presented in the courtroom.

The calculation of probabilities is strengthened through the use of Bayes' theorem in the calculation process (Aitken et al. 2010). A detailed description of Bayes' theorem is beyond the scope of this chapter; however, the use of Bayes' theorem to assist in explaining to the court mathematical or statistical assessments of probability has caused, and continues to cause, controversy in relation to expert evidence (Berger et al. 2011). The Appeal Court has issued guidance for practitioners, experts and the judiciary in English courts, where their concern is for the introduction of Bayes' theorem as evidence because of its potential to confuse the fact-finder and thus lead to miscarriages of justice. However, this approach has been the subject of debate and challenged in the academic literature which has presented a strong case for the use of Bayesian methods, or at the very least the use of a likelihood ratio, to remain as an admissible measure of evidential strength in courts (Berger et al. 2011; Donnelly 2005; Fenton and Neil 2011; Robertson et al. 2011).

Case law gives an insight into how Bayesian approaches to evidence have been used in the UK courts. In *R v Adams*,[14] Adams was accused of a rape after a DNA profile was obtained from an intimate swab after a rape. The victim had only had a brief glimpse of her attacker, and while she initially described the offender as being between 20 and 25 years of age, white and clean shaven, the victim was unable to identify Adams from a line-up, and Adams's girlfriend provided an alibi for the night of the attack. This meant that the only evidence that linked Adams to the attack was the DNA profile. In the first trial a statistician was brought into the court to explain to the jury how they might use a fully Bayesian approach when interpreting the strength of the DNA evidence that was being presented by the experts to the court (Donnelly 2005). The prosecution scientist having calculated a match probability of 1 in 200 million, the probability calculated was the chance that someone would match the discovered DNA profile if they were innocent. As already discussed, this is not the same as the probability that the accused was innocent, which is the misunderstanding that is the prosecutor's fallacy, or the possibility that they are innocent if they match the profile. While the jury was instructed in the use of Bayes' theorem to allow them to understand the probabilities at the culmination of the trial, Adams was found guilty. There was an appeal which was upheld on the basis that the judge should have given more advice to the jury about how to approach the statistics presented in the courtroom, if they did not wish to use Bayes' theorem to interpret the evidence placed before them. The appeal was upheld and a retrial ordered at which, again, the evidence was presented using Bayes' theorem. This time the judge asked the experts to come together to create a way of explaining how to apply Bayes' theorem in their decision-making process. Adams was found guilty a second time and a second appeal was unsuccessful; however, the court ruled heavily against the use of Bayes' theorem, endorsing the reservations expressed in the first appeal as follows: 'To introduce Bayes Theorem, or any similar methods, into a criminal trial plunges the jury into inappropriate and unnecessary realms of theory and complexity deflecting them from their proper task'. They continued: 'We regard the reliance on evidence of this kind in such cases as a recipe for confusion, misunderstanding and misjudgement, possibly even amongst counsel, but very probably among judges and, as we conclude, almost certainly among jurors'. The appeal judges also referred to the statistical evidence when they rejected the appeal, when they held:

> But the apparently objective numerical figures used in the theorem (Bayes') may conceal the element of judgement on which it entirely depends. More importantly for present purposes, however, whatever the merits or demerits of the Bayes theorem in mathematical or statistical assessments of probability, it seems to us that it is not appropriate for use in jury trial or as a means to assist the jury in their task. … More fundamentally, however, the attempt to determine guilt or innocence on the basis of a mathematical formula, applied to each separate piece of evidence, is simply inappropriate to the jury's task. Jurors evaluate evidence and reach a conclusion not by means of a formula, mathematical or otherwise, but by the joint application of their individual common sense and knowledge of the world to the evidence before them.

In terms of the evaluation of evidence, the appeal judges in *R v T*[15] came to a very similar decision. In this case, a critical part of the evidence was a footwear mark recovered from the crime scene, the size, the extent of the wear and any acquired damage in the form of a likelihood ratio. The value of the observation of the pattern was calculated from a database held by the forensic science provider. The value of the size of the footwear was calculated from a database held by the Shoe and Allied Trade Association; however, the wear extent and damage were based on figures drawn simply from the experience of the expert. This gave a likelihood ratio of 100. This was presented as being a 'moderate degree' of scientific evidence to support the view that the trainers recovered from the defendant had made the marks in question.

The appeal that followed was based on the argument that the statistical evidence used by the expert was inherently unreliable. The appeal was upheld on a number of counts; first, the judges felt that any and all probabilistic evidence should be based upon a firm statistical basis, rather than a subjective view based on experience. In presenting this opinion they stated, 'An approach based on mathematical calculations is only as good as the reliability of the data used', and 'it is evident from the way in which XXX identified the figures to be used in the formula for pattern and size that none has any degree of precision'. Second, they argued that any statistics that are placed before the court have to be based on transparent calculations which can be debated and discussed in the open courtroom.

The findings of the Appeal Court in *R v T* have resulted in ongoing discussions in the literature on the use of Bayesian approaches to expert evidence evaluation and presentation with many claiming, as was the case post *R v Adams*,[16] that the court had misunderstood the likelihood ratio since this is necessarily based on measurements, but it is the fuller Bayesian analysis which can include subjective reasoning. However, if the expert chooses to utilise a Bayesian approach, the one part of the *R v T* judgement which should be emphasised is the importance of ensuring that the basis for any opinion should be made clear and placed in front of the court to allow the suppositions and reasoning to be explored during the court process.

Much of how an expert witness should report statistical evidence depends upon the expert's duty to assist a court. This has been addressed in other chapters in this volume and in legislation and the rulings of the England and Wales Court of Appeal, which has written much on what an expert witness should do and how they should do it. To reiterate, broadly an expert witness should assist a court whenever evidence is brought before that court which is beyond the 'competence of ordinary judges and jurors' to understand the significance of that case of that evidence. In the case where an expert may be asked to comment on some area of their expertise which is statistical, there are a few precise dividing lines to tell us when a more general expertise becomes the sort of structured knowledge accepted by a court as expert knowledge.

In a case of the supply of a controlled substance, methylenedioxyamphetamine (MDA),[17] Mr P, a long-term worker for a drug advice charity, testified on the amount of MDA claimed by a suspect to be for their own personal use. Mr P's evidence was based upon interviews with MDA users and upon his extensive working experience rather than any systematic or statistically based survey of MDA users. The prosecution claimed that his evidence was hearsay and should be excluded as a consequence, a claim that was upheld by the judge. In this case, the Court of Appeal took the line that data used to support an argument should be based upon an explicitly realised database and in a form by which 'any enquiring individual can examine and be propelled by the sheer weight of the observations in those data, to the same or very similar conclusions'.[18] This reflects the arguments put forward by the National Academy of Sciences (NAS) report, which exposes the lack of empirical support for much forensic science.

For statistical evidence, or evidence for which there is some element of uncertainty, the line between when statistical expertise is needed and when it is not can be very fine. In a drug supply case from the north of England[19] the prosecution expert gave evidence in a case involving the communality of telephone calls between the suspects. The appeal case contended that the prosecution expert, Mr H, a data analysist working for Northumbria Constabulary, was not an expert in telecommunications traffic and that no such expertise was required to 'collect and collate the mass of material in order to start to form a judgement on what conclusions might be gleaned from it'.

The problem for statistical evidence is that what is clearly in the realm of the statistician and what is within the expertise of the expert forensic scientist changes with time. A relatively early DNA case where a crime scene DNA profile was compared to DNA taken from a blood sample found[20] it 'appropriate for the statistician to expound to the jury and statistical approach for evaluating the likelihood that the defendant left the crime stain'. This would now be regarded as a routine evaluation of the DNA evidence with standard and accepted methods for conducting the calculations based on large databases requiring a suitable expert on forensic DNA and not a statistical expert.

What can be expected to be part of the expertise of an ordinary person is also far from clear-cut. For instance, where some arithmetic may be involved it is not necessary to call for the expertise of a mathematician since simple addition, subtraction and multiplication are known to all who have undertaken a standard education. Similarly, all forensic scientists should know and be comfortable explaining those statistical methods pertinent to their particular discipline within the forensic sciences. But when does the expertise become a specialist statistical expertise rather than a sound familiarity with the statistics required and commonly utilised? We would not wish to create a legal environment where a member of the London Mathematical Society had to testify in court when some simple arithmetic operation were required, nor should a fellow of the Royal Statistical Society be needed when a basic t-test is conducted as these should be easily within the grasp and expertise of any scientist. However, clearly in the case of Sally Clark, the expertise needed was that of a statistician who was familiar with a little paediatrics rather than a paediatrician who was struggling with the sometimes difficult and abstract ideas of the statistical sciences.

The Appeal Court in a case involving an unquantified identification based on facial mapping[21] took its lead from Lord Justice Hughes:[22]

> An expert who spends years studying this kind of comparison can properly form a judgement as to the significance of what he has found in any

> particular case. It is a judgement based on his experiences. A jury is entitled to be informed of his assessment. The alternative, of simply leaving the jury to make up his own mind about the similarities and dissimilarities, with no assistance at all about their significance, would be to give the jury raw material with no means of evaluating it. It would be likely to result in over-valuation of the evidence as under-valuation. It would be more, not less, likely to result in an unsafe conclusion than providing the jury with the expert's opinion, properly debated through cross examination and, if not shared by another expert, countered by contrary evidence.

However, that is not to say that an expert can simply give unsupported opinion. In a burglary case in which footwear marks were used as evidence, the Court of Appeal stated:[23]

> If a footwear examiner expressed a view that went beyond saying that the footwear could or could not make the mark concerned, the report should make it clear that the view is subjective and based on experience of the examiner, so that words such as 'scientific' used in making evaluations should not in fact be used because they would, before a jury, give an impression of a degree of precision and objectivity which is not present given the current state of expertise. The factors that the expert does use should, however, be set out and explained.

These two quotes seem to place the English Court of Appeal and, as a consequence, the other lower courts into a contradictory position as to what the expert is permitted to comment on. Should the expert seek to tell the court nothing but a fully worked demonstration of the facts in any matter with each and every observation placed into a context given by a systematically collected database, or should the expert give an opinion as to the relevance of the forensic observations based upon their collected experience and expertise of those same observations?

The answer from the courts appears to be either but not both. Some mixture of subjective although expert opinion and data from harder sources seems to be what the Appeal Court has objected to in the cases of both *R v Adams* and *R v T*. Both cases have brought an unhelpful notoriety to Bayesian approaches to evidence evaluation.

In both the attempt was made to combine the accumulation but unquantified experience of an expert with figures from a systematically collected database. These attempts have, for the respective courts under which the cases were heard, been considered problematic. The court expected to hear either expert opinion or expert comment upon the facts. The combination of both seems to have caused some evidential dilemma within the court causing a rejection of the expertise, a rejection of the evidence and ultimately the quashing of the case due to the confusion between matters of opinion and matters of fact. This is a great pity; however, more recent rulings in

R v Dlugosz, *R v Pickering* and *R v MDS*[24] by the Court of Appeal show that there is some flexibility in the way in which the court approaches these issues.

Modern statistical methods such as acyclic directed graphs, otherwise known as Bayesian networks, allow the combination of disparate observations from many sources in a single graph to give an evaluation of the totality of the evidence in a case (Taroni et al. 2014). Through use of a Bayesian network, it is easy to combine in an intellectually satisfying way likelihoods from some database of, say, frequencies of tool types, or gun primer compositions, and probabilities of seeing a given tool type, or primer composition, in a particular context from the accumulated experience of an expert with many years of experience. The mathematics of a Bayesian network do not necessarily distinguish between the two. The process can, in some circumstances, be quite simple, and the calculations conducted using sophisticated software. This sort of treatment of multifaceted observations is, from the statistical point of view, and if the networks themselves are sufficiently well constructed, unproblematic.

In some ways it is easy to understand the suspicion of courts towards Bayesian networks and other related methods for evaluating evidence. Although it is possible in principle to take a software-based Bayesian network and work each stage of the propagation of information throughout the network by manual means, for any real network the process would be very time-consuming, possibly to the extent of being outside the time frame of a trial. Some aspects of the use of Bayesian networks might worry a court for other reasons. The use of a computer system for the calculations involved in any network other than the most trivial is more or less necessary. So the output of a Bayesian network might seem like the output from a 'black box' to the court, and it might seem that the inner workings of it are not subject to the sort of explicit, detailed, and open scrutiny expected of evidence being brought into criminal, or civil, proceedings. Additional concerns might come about because the output from a Bayesian network is always numeric and might, to the lay examiner, give the impression of a spurious precision because, although all uncertainties from any combination of unquantified expertise and precise estimates from systematically collected databases are taken into account, the numeric output will remain of the same form and order of precision irrespective of whether most of the likelihoods in the network are based upon expert intuitions or large databases. The very ease with which Bayesian networks can be employed to provide numeric evaluations for evidence can lend itself to their use by the inexperienced. If any court is itself unable to assess the analysis undertaken in any Bayesian network, then any poorly constructed or ill-conceived network will give a potentially misleading evaluation and interpretation of the evidence in a case. The same may be said of modern software (Chikkagoudar et al. 2011) designed to untangle and evaluate DNA mixtures. Again, we come back to the matter of evidence, and its evaluation, being open and publicly demonstrable, rather than something which cannot be brought before the general public.

The current position in the English and Welsh courts, despite statistical methods existing which allow for the combination of different evidence types, is that the expert who may have many years of experience in an area of forensic science, and may have seen many more instances, and observed many more features of a material of forensic significance than exist in systematically collected databases, should only provide an unquantified opinion of the meaning of their observations. This is because the data upon which they base their opinion exists only as a set of memories and cannot be held up to public examination in the same way that a numerically inferior, less complete, but systematically recorded database can be.

In principle the most convincing and highest-quality expert evidence is that which is given as testimony to fact, where each and every statement is supported by an appeal to the sort of structured observations which exist in systematically collected databases. So long as the entries in the database are trusted, and the reasoning is clear, the process is fully accountable and will fulfill the public scrutiny aspects of both science and the law. For those areas of expertise which are often used, and for which the data exist, and for which the statistical methods are established, the statistical evaluation of forensic evidence is, or should be, routine.

However, there are clearly problems implementing this quality of evidential evaluation across all forms of forensic and legal evidence. Databases of all possible entities and all possible materials just do not exist, and are unlikely to ever do so. In some circumstances a statistical expert can work with the scientific expert to identify the best way of evaluating the evidence, and the best data upon which to base that evaluation. Unfortunately, in others any further quantitative work may not be possible due to the absence of a suitably collected set of data. In these cases the expert will have to testify as to their opinion, rather than fact. Any attempt to mix a testimony of fact and a testimony of opinion, using some form of Bayesian approach in whatever form, has in the past been regarded with suspicion by the court, and led to the sorts of controversial rulings seen in *R v Adams* and *R v T*, which would appear to undermine the use of Bayesian reasoning throughout United Kingdom jurisdictions; however, rulings such as those given in *R v Dlugosz*[25] by the Court of Appeal demonstrate that this is not always the case and that courts can demonstrate a degree of flexibility in relation to the evidence placed before it. In each case the Court of Appeal felt that this evidence was admissible in specific circumstances so long as the limitations of the evidence were made clear to the court and the jury so that they could make their own decisions on the strength of the evidence. It is of interest that again the appeal judges stressed the importance of ensuring that the jury was given all of the facts and that the arguments were transparent and clearly made.

Just who is an expert in statistics, and just how much statistical science is part of the common competence of a forensic expert, is, and will always be, in flux. For evidence types for which established statistical methods exist, such as many DNA evidence problems, the evaluation, reporting and presentation to the court should mostly be a matter of course, and can safely be seen as part of the competence of the DNA expert. For evidence where no firmly established statistical methods exist, the forensic expert needs to tread carefully. The handful of statistical methods taught to the scientific expert during the course of their undergraduate careers are unlikely to be sufficient to answer the sometimes difficult problems of statistical evidence evaluation. To be competent to a level adequate for the reporting of non-standard forensic evidence, the expert should be completely familiar and comfortable with ideas such as statistical independence and conditional probability. All experts, regardless of field of competence, specialism or profession, should heed the advice of Sir Anthony Clarke and Lord Justices Auld and Thorpe when quoting from a previous judgement in the Sally Clark case:[26] 'An expert witness should make it clear when a particular question or issue falls outside his expertise'.

Notes

1. See Court of Appeal judgements *R v Clark* (2000) EWCA Crim 54, 2 October 2000 and *R v Clark* (2003) EWCA Crim 1020, 11 April 2003 and *R v Adams* (1996) 2 Cr App R 467, (1996) Crim LR 898, CA and *R v Adams* (1998) 1 Cr App R 377.
2. See Jacobs, S. Judge tosses out two types of DNA evidence used regularly in criminal cases. *Daily News*, Jan 5. 2015. http://www.nydailynews.com/new-york/nyc-crime/judge-tosses-types-dna-testing-article-1.2065795.
3. See *R v Dlugosz*; *R v Pickering*; *R v MDS* (2013) All ER (D) 01 (Feb). http://www.statewatch.org/news/2014/sep/uk-dna-judgment-court-of-appeal-subjective-assessment-ruling.pdf.
4. *R v Turner* (1975) Q.B. 834, 841.
5. *R v T* (2010) All ER (D) 240 (Oct); (2010) EWCA Crim 2439.
6. See *R v Dlugosz*; *R v Pickering*; *R v MDS* (2013) All ER (D) 01 (Feb). http://www.statewatch.org/news/2014/sep/uk-dna-judgment-court-of-appeal-subjective-assessment-ruling.pdf.
7. See Court of Appeal judgements *R v Clark* (2000) EWCA Crim 54, 2 October 2000 and *R v Clark* (2003) EWCA Crim 1020, 11 April 2003.
8. *R v Watters* (2000) All ER (D) 1469.
9. *R v Hookway and Another* (2011) EWCA Crim 1986.
10. *R v Dallagher* (2002) EWCA Crim 1903 and *R v Kempster* (2008) All ER (D) 76.
11. *R v Otway* (2011) All ER (D) 75.
12. *R v Barry George* (2007) EWCA Crim 2722.
13. *R v Dodson and Williams* (1984) 79 Cr.
14. *R v Adams* (1996) 2 Cr App R 467, (1996) Crim LR 898, CA and *R v Adams* (1998) 1 Cr App R 377.

15. *R v T* (2010) All ER (D) 240 (Oct); (2010) EWCA Crim 2439.
16. *R v Adams* (1996) 2 Cr App R 467, (1996) Crim LR 898, CA and *R v Adams* (1998) 1 Cr App R 377.
17. *R v Edwards* (2001) All ER (D) 271.
18. *R v Edwards*, neutral citation number: 2185, 2001, EWCA Crim.
19. *R v Allsop and Others* (2005) EWCA Crim 703.
20. *R v Doheny, Adams* (1996) EWCA Crim 648, (1996) EWCA Crim 728, (1997) 1 Cr App R 369.
21. *R v Reed, Reed and Garmson* (2009) EWCA Crim 2698.
22. *R v Atkins & Atkins* (2009) EWCA Crim 1876, (2010) 1 Cr.
23. *R v T* (2010) All ER (D) 240 (Oct); (2010) EWCA Crim 2439.
24. See *R v Dlugosz; R v Pickering; R v MDS* (2013) All ER (D) 01 (Feb). http://www.statewatch.org/news/2014/sep/uk-dna-judgment-court-of-appeal-subjective-assessment-ruling.pdf.
25. See *R v Dlugosz; R v Pickering; R v MDS* (2013) All ER (D) 01 (Feb). http://www.statewatch.org/news/2014/sep/uk-dna-judgment-court-of-appeal-subjective-assessment-ruling.pdf.
26. See Court of Appeal judgements *R v Clark* (2000) EWCA Crim 54, 2 October 2000 and *R v Clark* (2003) EWCA Crim 1020, 11 April 2003.

References

Aitken, Colin G. G., and Franco Taroni. *Statistics and the Evaluation of Evidence for Forensic Scientists*. Vol. 16. Chichester: Wiley, 2004.

Aitken, Colin, Paul Roberts, and Graham Jackson. *Fundamentals of Probability and Statistical Evidence in Criminal Proceedings: Guidance for Judges, Lawyers, Forensic Scientists and Expert Witnesses*. London: Royal Statistical Society, 2010.

Balding, David J. Evaluation of mixed source, low-template DNA profiles in forensic science. *Proceedings of the National Academy of Sciences* 110, no. 30 (2013): 12241–12246.

Berger, Charles E. H., John Buckleton, Christophe Champod, Ian W. Evett, and Graham Jackson. Evidence evaluation: A response to the court of appeal judgment in *R v T. Science & Justice* 51, no. 2 (2011): 43–49.

Buchanan, Mark. Statistics: Conviction by numbers. *Nature* 445, no. 7125 (2007): 254–255.

Champod, Christophe. Identification and individualization. In *Wiley Encyclopedia of Forensic Science*. 2009.

Chikkagoudar, Satish, Kai Wang, and Mingyao Li. GENIE: A software package for gene-gene interaction analysis in genetic association studies using multiple GPU or CPU cores. *BMC Research Notes* 4, no. 1 (2011): 158.

Christensen, Angi M. The impact of *Daubert*: Implications for testimony and research in forensic anthropology (and the use of frontal sinuses in personal identification. *Journal of Forensic Sciences* 49, no. 3 (2004): 427–430.

Christensen, Angi M., Christian M. Crowder, Stephen D. Ousley, and Max M. Houck. Error and its meaning in forensic science. *Journal of Forensic Sciences* 59, no. 1 (2014): 123–126.

Dawid, Philip. Statistics and the law. *Nature* 428 (2004): 799.

Donnelly, Peter. Appealing statistics. *Significance* 2, no. 1 (2005): 46–48.

Fenton, Norman, and Martin Neil. Avoiding probabilistic reasoning fallacies in legal practice using Bayesian networks. *Australian Journal of Legal Philosophy* 36 (2011): 114.

Henderson, J. P. The use of DNA statistics in criminal trials. *Forensic Science International* 128, no. 3 (2002): 183–186.

Kaye, David H. Probability, individualization, and uniqueness in forensic science evidence: Listening to the academies. *Brooklyn Law Review* 75, no. 4 (2010): 1163–1185.

Knupfer, G. C. (Ed.). *Encyclopedia of Forensic Sciences*. London: Academic Press, (2000): pp. 1077–1083.

Koehler, Jonathan J., and David H. Kaye. Can jurors understand probabilistic evidence? *Journal of the Royal Statistical Society, Series A* 154, no. 1 (1991): 75–81.

Koehler, Jonathan J., and Michael J. Saks. Individualization claims in forensic science: Still unwarranted. *Brooklyn Law Review* 75 (2010): 1187.

Kuchler, Benoit, Christophe Champod, and Ian W. Evett. Earmarks as evidence: A critical review. *Journal of Forensic Science* 46, no. 6 (2001): 1275–1284.

Law Commission. Expert evidence in criminal proceedings in England and Wales. 2011.

Lord Thomas of Cwngiedd. Expert evidence: The future of forensic science in criminal trials. The 2014 Criminal Bar Association, Kalisher lecture. 2014. https://www.judiciary.gov.uk/wp-content/uploads/2014/10/kalisher-lecture-expert-evidence-oct-14.pdf [accessed on 31/06/2016].

National Research Council. Strengthening forensic science in the United States: A path forward. 2009.

Nobles, Richard, and David Schiff. Misleading statistics within criminal trials. *Significance* 2, no. 1 (2005): 17–19.

Page, Mark, Jane Taylor, and Matt Blenkin. Uniqueness in the forensic identification sciences – Fact or fiction? *Forensic Science International* 206, no. 1 (2011): 12–18.

Redmayne, Mike. Presenting probabilities in court: The DNA experience. *International Journal of Evidence & Proof* 1 (1996): 187.

Robertson, Bernard, G. A. Vignaux, and Charles E. H. Berger. Extending the confusion about Bayes. *The Modern Law Review* 74, no. 3 (2011): 444–455.

Saks, Michael J., and Jonathan J. Koehler. The coming paradigm shift in forensic identification science. *Science* 309, no. 5736 (2005): 892–895.

Saks, Michael J., and Jonathan J. Koehler. The individualization fallacy in forensic science evidence. *Vanderbilt Law Review* 61, no. 1 (2008): 199–219.

Saks, Michael J., and Jonathan J. Koehler. What DNA fingerprinting can teach the law about the rest of forensic science. *Cardozo Law Review* 13 (1991): 361.

Scotland Fingerprint Inquiry. The Fingerprint Inquiry report. Edinburgh: APS Group Scotland, 2011.

Taroni, Franco, Alex Biedermann, Silvia Bozza, Paolo Garbolino, and Colin Aitken. *Bayesian Networks for Probabilistic Inference and Decision Analysis in Forensic Science*. Chichester: John Wiley & Sons, 2014.

9 The Expert Witness in the Inquisitorial Justice System Compared with the Adversarial Systems of the UK*

VERENA MURSCHETZ

Contents

9.1 Introduction

The purpose of this chapter is to give an overview on the use of experts in inquisitorial justice systems, exemplified by the Austrian model. In order to allow for a comprehensive understanding of the role of experts, the general differences between adversarial and inquisitorial systems need to be demonstrated first. Accordingly, the chapter provides a general comparison of the two systems in Section 9.2. Section 9.3 explains the Austrian pre-trial

* This chapter was submitted in 2015.

and trial phase as an example of an inquisitorial prosecution system. Section 9.4 deals with the expert in the Austrian criminal proceedings. The role of the expert, the selection process, qualifications and challenges are addressed. The chapter shows that the Austrian law on expert testimony in criminal cases does not qualify as a role model, as it does not provide the defendant with sufficient tools to achieve equality of arms in the process.

9.2 Inquisitorial versus Adversarial Process – An Overview

While common law countries, such as England and Scotland, use the adversarial process in criminal proceedings, most European civil law countries, such as, for example, Austria, Germany, France and Switzerland, adopt an inquisitorial process. The term 'inquisitorial' is hardly used by continental European scholars, though, due to the negative connotation of its medieval forebear. To distinguish the trial process from this classic medieval inquisitorial system, it is often described as accusatorial or 'akkusatorisch' in German.[1] An exception to the mainly inquisitorial systems in European civil law countries is Italy, which abolished the inquisitorial trial in 1988 and introduced an adversarial process fashioned after the U.S. American model.[2]

What has to be clarified, though, is that this clearly defined theoretical categorization in inquisitorial and adversarial trials or systems does not necessarily exist in reality in the legal systems of the world, even though it will be used throughout this chapter. Rather, those categories represent ideal models that are in practice not designed uniformly. Still, the systems which can be allocated to one ideal model are very similar regarding their main elements, especially the role the parties and the judge play in the procedural discovery of evidence, the admissibility of hearsay evidence and the general requirement of independent and direct fact-finding through oral evidence presented at trial.[3]

The adversarial trial relies mostly on the skills of the advocates for the 'parties'. The procedural discovery of the evidence is in their hands and they are therefore given equal opportunity to present their side of the case. Consequently, it is their job to convince the fact-finder of the truth of their story. This fact-finder in the adversarial trial is a jury or a judge. The judge's responsibility is to make sure that the process is conducted fairly, that due process prevails. Civil lawyers often criticize that the purpose of an adversarial trial is only to find out the 'formal' truth as established by the two parties.[4]

The inquisitorial system, on the other hand, relies not on the skills of the attorneys but on the skills of the judge, as a neutral and objective person. The main player during the trial is the judge, not the parties; the procedural discovery of the evidence is in the judge's hands. It is his or her job to establish the facts, to find out the truth and to deliver the verdict. The parties have a right to ask additional questions once the judge has finished questioning. Jury trials are very limited, applicable in the most severe cases only, such as crimes with a possible punishment of lifelong imprisonment or at least a minimal sentence of more than 5 and a maximum of more than 10 years imprisonment,[5] and are always still under the control of the judge.[6] Those civil lawyers who criticize the mere 'formal' truth-finding in adversarial systems like to stress that the inquisitorial system achieves a higher goal, that is, to find out the 'material truth', the real truth, instead of the formal truth as established by the parties only.[7]

9.3 The Austrian Prosecution System as an Example of an Inquisitorial Model

9.3.1 Pre-Trial Phase

In order to allow for an evaluation of the use of expert witnesses in the inquisitorial system, a brief outline of the pre-trial and trial proceedings is essential. While many inquisitorial systems use an 'investigative judge' as the decision maker in the pre-trial proceedings, Austrian law has abolished this institution in 2008 in favour of a strong prosecutor. The prosecutor is in charge of the pre-trial proceedings and as such solely competent to assign and instruct an expert, if he or she lacks the necessary knowledge.[8] Prosecutors are considered judicial organs by the constitution. As such prosecutors are (theoretically) regarded as neutral and objective and are trusted to weigh up the case for both sides. They are required to look for and take into account not only incriminating but also exculpatory evidence.[9] In practice of course, the police conduct most investigations independently. They present the prosecutor with completed files at the conclusion of the investigation. Contact occurs earlier if the police consider the assistance of an expert necessary or wish to exercise coercive powers that require formal prosecutorial orders and judicial warrants. Once police close the investigations, they hand the files over to the prosecutors, who then decide whether to prosecute.[10] The judge in the pre-trial investigatory phase is given the role of an independent arbiter. He or she rules on challenges against the selection and assignment of an expert by the prosecutor in the pre-trial phase. The judge also decides on requests by the police or prosecutors to employ coercive measures,[11] such as search, surveillance and pre-trial detention.[12]

The importance of this pre-trial phase needs to be emphasized, when discussing the inquisitorial system. During this pre-trial phase, all relevant evidence is gathered and collected in the so-called case dossier, the case file. It contains all the evidence considered important, including the findings of experts, who in practice are mostly assigned in the pre-trial phase.

All witness statements, background information, the criminal record of the accused, and so on, are also collected in the file.[13] The witness statements (not the findings of the expert) are prepared by the police, who conduct pre-trial questioning, write down witnesses' statements and have them signed by the witnesses. Video- and audio-taping of the testimony is not mandatory and therefore not used in practice. No specific rules of evidence apply. So long as information is relevant, it may be presented in the dossier.[14] During this clearly inquisitorial pre-trial investigation phase, equality of arms does not exist and the rights of the accused are not adequately protected. Police and the prosecutor play the active roles. The procurement of evidence is in their hands. The prosecutor selects, assigns and instructs the expert. During the questioning by the police, generally neither the accused nor defence counsel have a right to be present or to ask questions. The limits on the selection of the experts will be discussed in the next section. Once the prosecutor decides to bring charges, the whole dossier is filed with the charges. Hence, the judge, who presides over the case, is handed over all this information.

9.3.2 Trial Phase

9.3.2.1 Principles Guiding the Trial Phase

Once the file reaches the court, judges control the case. They set trial dates and based on the case file they call the relevant witnesses and assign the experts they deem necessary.[15] The procurement of the evidence at trial is in the hands of the judges. They conduct the questioning of the witnesses and of the experts. Therefore, the job of the judge during the trial is to investigate, find the facts and decide the case as well as to act as a referee, four functions which are not necessarily compatible. In particular, giving the investigation and fact-finding power to one person is problematic. If the parties criticize the investigation, that is, questioning undertaken by the judge, they implicitly criticize not just the investigator but also the fact-finder.

In order to be able to prepare for and conduct the trial, especially to carry out the questioning, inquisitorial systems consider it indispensable that judges are handed the pre-trial case dossier. Consequently, they study thoroughly this file containing all relevant evidence, including expert findings and opinions, witness statements, and so on. Of course, this knowledge of the file poses the danger that the trial itself and the verdict rely merely on written pre-trial statements. In order to (at least theoretically) distance the fact-finding from the written statements, allow a fair process and grant the accused the right to confront the witnesses against himself or herself, the trial is supposed to operate on the principles of 'orality' and 'immediacy'. All evidence has to be presented orally in court and the immediate or first-hand evidence, rather than written statements, needs to be presented at trial. Therefore, the expert needs to appear at the hearing and deliver his or her opinion orally. Thus, in principle judges should find the facts and decide the case on the basis of oral evidence presented in court only, and not on the basis of the statements contained in the pre-trial dossier.[16] In practice, this is of course hard to achieve. The real risk exists that judges merely strive for the confirmation of the hypothesis they have formed by reading the case file.[17]

9.3.2.2 Presentation of Evidence

Testimony during the trial is not guided by the parties, but the judge. The judge carries out the questioning of experts and witnesses. Prosecuting and defence lawyers only have a right to ask questions once the judge is done and gives them the floor. Consequently, the questioning by the parties is conducted in a manner very different from an adversarial system. Specifically, the questioning by the defence is a lot less confrontational because too aggressive or merely too lengthy questioning might suggest that the judge was not conducting the trial properly. This could have harmful consequences for the outcome of the case. As the trial judge is not just the person gathering the evidence during the trial but also the ultimate fact-finder, any kind of (implied) critique might be harmful for the defence. Because the procedural discovery is in the hands of the judge and the judge conducts the questioning, no formal distinction exists between prosecution and defence witnesses; they are all 'judges' witnesses. Experts are not presented by the parties but the judges and are therefore questioned by the judge as court-appointed specialists. Regarding the questioning itself, no distinction between examination-in-chief and cross-examination exists. Rather, evidence is supposed to be presented in the form of a narrative, with witnesses allowed to recount events without significant interruption by the judges or the parties. The reasoning is that the witness is questioned by a person operating from a neutral standpoint, whose main concern is to get the person to tell the truth, instead of a party who tries to convince the fact-finder that the witness lacks credibility.[18] Of course, as noted earlier, the neutral judge might already have formed a preconception by studying the case file and therefore might merely aim to achieve a confirmation of this hypothesis.[19]

Other than in adversarial systems hardly any evidentiary rules apply. There is no need for corroboration and there is no hearsay rule. Also, the highly relevant distinction between evidence of factual matters and evidence of opinion made in English and Scottish law does not exist.[20] All relevant evidence is to be used. Fact-finding is guided by the principle of 'free assessment of evidence': judges ought to be directed only by scientific knowledge and the principles of logic and common sense in the evaluation of the evidence presented.[21] This is the case because judges are trusted to weigh the evidence correctly, to make the required distinctions between hearsay and immediate evidence, or between trustworthy and unreliable evidence.

In the end the judge decides upon guilt or innocence of the accused and the sentence. This is done in one hearing. The verdict can be an acquittal or a conviction. Both have to be reasoned and can be appealed by both the prosecution and the defence.

9.4 The Use of Experts in the Austrian Inquisitorial Process

9.4.1 Definition and Role of the Expert in the Inquisitorial Process

Now that the proceedings in general have been outlined, the role of experts, the selection process, questions of competence and objectivity, as well as possible challenges, will be presented. First, in inquisitorial systems 'expert witness' is, strictly speaking, not the correct term, because experts are not witnesses. The term 'expert witness' (*sachverständiger Zeuge* in German) does exist (even though not recognized by the Austrian Code of Criminal Procedure), but it identifies something different. An expert witness is an ordinary witness who has specific knowledge in the field, and whose testimony might be given more weight by the fact-finder. If, for instance, a police officer witnesses a car accident, his or her testimony might be valued more because the judge might assume that due to her education and training she might have a more comprehensive and understanding perceptivity of the circumstances of the accident.[22] Experts, on the other hand, are not witnesses. The Austrian code defines an expert as a person who, due to her special knowledge in the specific field, is able to determine relevant facts, the so-called factual findings (*Befund*), or is able to draw legally relevant and reasoned conclusions from these findings, the so-called expert opinion (*Gutachten*).[23] Experts are supposed to be neutral and objective.[24] They are assigned individually by the prosecutor during the investigative pre-trial proceedings or the judge at trial, if the facts lie beyond the understanding of the prosecutor or the court, such as mental illness, the degree of an injury, and so on. The expert therefore has a particular knowledge in a specific field that police, prosecutor or judge are lacking and substitutes this missing expertise. Therefore, the following characteristics apply to experts: they are ordered by the prosecutor (before trial) or by the court, are advisory in nature and are used to benefit the (supposedly objective) prosecutor in the pre-trial phase and the judge in the trial phase, and neither are bound to the findings of the expert.[25] In addition, the expert should only give factual advice, never any legal opinion. The judge must carry out the legal evaluation of the facts independently. Of course, this is a somewhat grey area and sometimes the distinction between prohibited legal conclusions or opinions and subject-specific conclusions or opinions are hard to draw.[26] What has been under discussion is the role of the expert in relation to the judge. Experts have the right to be present during (non-public) pre-trial or trial interrogations or questionings of witnesses, and the accused may ask questions themselves. Additionally, in a sense they substitute the knowledge which the judge is lacking, such as regarding the existence and level of a mental illness. Therefore, it has been questioned whether experts are subsidiary organs to the court or if they are simply giving ordinary evidence. The general understanding is that their expert contribution is part of the evidence just like witnesses and exhibits and as such is subject to the rule of free evaluation of evidence,[27] meaning that judges are free to trust the expertise or not. In practice of course, as experts substitute the missing special knowledge of the court, they do enjoy a special position. Because the judge lacks the expertise, he or she will mostly not be in a position to carry out a 'quality control' regarding the findings or opinions of the expert. What is left is a mere plausibility control by the courts and a de facto tie to the expert opinion.[28] Limited challenges are possible and are discussed in Section 9.4.2.3. The danger of miscarriages of justice, which exists in all systems, might be reduced in the Austrian system by the statutory qualification requirements[29] and the certification process for experts. The fact that the expert is hired by the court and not by the parties might also reduce this risk. However, the endorsement of the (pre-trial) expert assigned and instructed by the prosecutor for the trial proceedings by the judge might pose an obstacle to objectivity. This specific problem is addressed in the next section.

9.4.2 Selection of the Expert in the Pre-Trial and Trial Phase

9.4.2.1 Selection Process

The selection process differs greatly from the common law legal systems, including those in England and Scotland. In the pre-trial phase the prosecutor as the head of the proceedings is in charge of selecting and assigning the expert, if either police or the prosecutor lack the required knowledge. If the prosecutor files charges, the indictment is usually supported by this expert testimony. At the trial stage, the judge selects and commissions the expert. The trial judge is free to commission the 'pre-trial' expert, the expert who has already been assigned by the prosecutor in the pre-trial phase. This is what happens in practice.[30] The problem associated with this practice is of course that at the trial the prosecutor becomes a party, an adversary. Consequently, the expert assigned and instructed by this party in the trial proceedings becomes the expert of the judge. One might ask if this is in line with the requirements of a fair trial. It could be argued that the findings and opinion of an expert selected by the adversary amount to evidence against the defendant.[31] The law does not consider this as a problem, though. The mere fact that the expert has been assigned, instructed and 'used' by the prosecution in the pre-trial investigative phase, and therefore by the adversary in the trial proceedings, explicitly does not constitute partiality and does not allow for a challenge.[32] The accused has the general right to challenge the selection of the expert on grounds of partiality or lacking competence and may name a more qualified person. However, as mentioned, the endorsement or re-assignment of the (pre-trial) expert expressly does not amount to partiality.

9.4.2.2 Qualifications

The required qualifications of experts are listed in the code of experts and interpreters (SDG).[33] Generally, expertise and knowledge, professionalism and objectivity are essential. In order to allow for an easier selection of qualified and suitable persons the code requires a list of court-certified experts for the jurisdiction of each regional appellate court, who have also been placed under oath. It is the task of the presidents of the regional appellate courts to administer this list and assess and certify the individual experts regarding their field of competence. The list is published on the web page of the ministry of justice.[34] The understanding is that once an expert is court certified and listed, the requirements of expertise, professionalism and objectivity are met. Because of this rebuttable assumption, there is no need to establish individual competence in the field in each case. Prosecutors or the courts are not obliged to select the expert from this list, but mostly do so in practice. Apart from competence and qualification, prosecutors and judges are required to apply the principles of austerity, economic efficiency and practicability to the selection process. The cost of the state-appointed expert has to been borne by the defendant in the case of a conviction.

Overall, it is seen as the task of the prosecutor and the judge to select an objective expert best qualified for the job. What happens a lot in practice, though, is the continuous assignment of experts with whom prosecutors or courts have worked well before. This could have a negative connotation of course, if the good relationship exists because the expert delivers the answers the prosecutor/judge wished for.[35]

9.4.2.3 Challenges

The accused/defendant has a right to challenge the appointment of the expert on the grounds of partiality or incompetence. The reasons establishing partiality are those applying to police officers and prosecutors as well.[36] Among other expressly listed grounds, the code contains a general provision stating reasons that raise doubt regarding the full objectivity and impartiality of the expert. As mentioned before, a challenge on the grounds of partiality may not be based on the fact that the expert assigned by the trial court is the same person that had been assigned, instructed and guided as an expert in the pretrial phase by the prosecutor, who now represents the adversary. This double function of the expert as an expert for the prosecutor and the judge expressly does not constitute bias.[37] From the viewpoint of an adversarial lawyer, the justification and validity of this model must be quite questionable. It raises serious doubts in the Austrian justice system as well. As the defendant is not granted the full opportunity to use his or her own expert for the defence, the principle of equality of rights is clearly not implemented. The following section discusses the restrictions applying to such experts for the defence.

9.4.3 The Role of Experts for the Defence

As mentioned in Section 9.3.2, inquisitorial systems do not put the procurement of evidence at trial in the hands of the parties but in the hands of the judge. The investigative pre-trial phase is under the supervision of the prosecutor. Therefore, at this stage it is the prosecutor's task to select and instruct an expert. Of course, at this stage the defendant is free to hire a person with special knowledge to help with his or her defence. However, this person does not have any special standing at trial. He or she does not have the status of an expert and is therefore not recognized as such by the trial judge. The defendant's expert may therefore not be present at (non-public) interrogations or questionings of witnesses. At trial, the expert for the defence will not be heard as an expert. Only the court-appointed expert acts as an expert and is therefore entitled and required to deliver the expert opinion orally. Of course, the defendant may file a motion to have the expert for the defence heard as a mere witness. The expert opinion will not be heard by the court and not become part of the relevant evidence. The only right explicitly granted to the defence by law is the right to use a private expert for the questioning of the court-appointed expert. As mentioned before, the court-appointed expert needs to present his or her expert opinion orally at trial. According to the procedure outlined in Section 9.3.2, the judge conducts the questioning of the expert. Once the judge has finished, the parties are allowed to pose additional questions. (Only) since 2015 have experts for the defence themselves been able to ask the court-appointed expert questions regarding their findings and orally presented expert opinion. Through this tool they might be able to test competence or objectivity. Of course the judge does not need to follow up on the issues raised, but he or she might order the expert to revise the opinion. Such concerns raised do not usually result in the appointment of the expert for the defence as court expert, though.

Also, until the revision of the 2015 law, the courts held that opinions of experts for the defence were not part of the relevant evidence, and could therefore be ignored.[38] The reasoning behind this is, as stated before, that only the court-appointed expert can deliver expert opinions, whereas experts of the defence are mere witnesses and can therefore only give evidence about observations they made (just like other witnesses). Consequently, the verdict cannot be appealed on the ground that it ignored the defence expert's opinion. As the revision of the code has not clarified this issue, it is quite likely that courts will adhere to their prior rulings. In summary it can be said that at trial the main task of the expert for the defence is to assist the defendant in testing the competence of the court-appointed expert. His or her expert opinions, however, do not constitute expert testimony and can be ignored completely. Only direct observations of the defence expert as a witness can be introduced as evidence.

9.5 Conclusion

As in the UK systems, the role of the expert in the inquisitorial systems is to provide the necessary scientific criteria to the trier of fact to allow them to make an informed and independent judgement of facts. Experts do not need to establish or demonstrate their competence in the field in each case, though. They are rather court certified and sworn in and as such featured on a list by the president of each regional appellate court. This monitoring mechanism is supposed to control the issues of competence sufficiently. Of course, a challenge on grounds of incompetence can be brought forward. Furthermore, as the procurement of evidence at trial is in the hands of the judge and not the parties in inquisitorial proceedings, experts are assigned and instructed by the judge and have a duty to the judge only. As such, experts are considered objective and independent advisors to the courts. Consequently, the danger voiced by representatives of adversarial systems such as the UK, of experts appearing as hired guns for each side, does not seem to exist in inquisitorial systems. However, the Austrian system does not qualify as the model for change. Defendants have to deal with the fact that the expert, who has been selected, assigned and instructed by the prosecution in the investigative pre-trial phase, is the expert testifying at trial as well, as courts generally confirm the pre-trial experts. The competence of the prosecutor to select, assign and pose the relevant questions to the expert, who will then deliver the findings and opinions to the judge at trial, exists because the prosecutor is institutionally in charge of the pre-trial phase. As the head of (inquisitorial) pre-trial proceedings the prosecutor is considered neutral and objective and therefore qualified to select and instruct experts without bias. Their status as an (independent) judicial organ is even constitutionally foreseen. At trial, on the other hand, the prosecutor represents the state as the accuser, the person asking for the prosecution and conviction of the defendant. Consequently, the expert presenting his or her opinion at trial has been selected, instructed and guided up until the beginning of the trial by the prosecutor now representing the adversary. This fact alone is expressly not considered to give grounds for a challenge of partiality. The reasonableness and validity of this model is questionable from many viewpoints, including due process and equality of arms. These concerns are further validated by the fact that the findings and expert opinion of a specialist hired by the defence do not constitute expert testimony. A change of the Austrian law towards a more adversarial perspective is needed.

Notes

1. Ryan, A. 2014. *Towards a System of European Criminal Justice: The Problem of Admissibility of Evidence*, 68. Oxon: Routledge.
2. See Grande, E. 2000. Italian criminal justice: Borrowing and resistance. *American Journal of Comparative Law* 48: 227. Murschetz, V. 2015. Reform der Hauptverhandlung - adversatorische versus inquisitorische Hauptverhandlung. In *13. Österreichischer StrafverteidigerInnentag*, ed. R. Soyer. Wien: NWV – Neuer Wissenschaftlicher Verlag.
3. Hörnle, T. 2005. Unterschiede zwischen Strafverfahrensordnungen und ihre kulturellen Hintergründe. *ZStW* 117: 801–804. Murschetz, V. 2015. Reform der Hauptverhandlung - adversatorische versus inquisitorische Hauptverhandlung. In *13. Österreichsicher StrafverteidigerInnentag*, ed. R. Soyer. Wien: NWV – neuer Wissenschaftlicher Verlag.
4. For a discussion see Weßlau, E. 2014. Wahrheit und Legenden: die Debatte über den adversatorischen Strafprozess, *ZIS* 11/2014, 558 ff.
5. § 31 (2) Code of Criminal Procedure.
6. Murschetz, V. 2009. The U.S. jury system: An insight from a civil lawyer's perspective. In *Legal Narratives: European Perspectives on U.S. Law in Cultural Context*, ed. A. Gamper and G. M. Grabher, 168 f, 171 f. Heidelberg: Springer-Verlag.
7. For a discussion see Murschetz, V. 2015. Reform der Hauptverhandlung – adversatorische versus inquisitorische Hauptverhandlung. In *13. Österreichischer StrafverteidigerInnentag*, ed. R. Soyer. Wien: NWV – neuer Wissenschaftlicher Verlag. Weßlau, E. 2014. Wahrheit und Legenden: die Debatte über den adversatorischen Strafprozess. *ZIS* 11/2014, 558 ff.
8. The role of the expert is discussed in Section 9.4.1.
9. Murschetz, V. 2012. Child witnesses in Austria. In *Children and Cross-Examination – Time to Change the Rules?* ed J. R. Spencer, and M. E. Lamb, 132. Oxford: Hart Publishing Ltd. Fabrizy, E. E. 2014. *Strafprozessordnung*, 37. Wien: Manz Verlag.
10. The defence have a right to access the file and can request further lines of investigation or the questioning of additional witnesses. Prosecutors or police are obliged to act on such requests, carrying them out or denying them, with the defence having right to appeal denials to the court; see Bertel, C. and A. Venier. 2014. *Strafprozessrecht*, 114, 119, 121–132. Wien: Manz Verlag.
11. Code of Criminal Procedure Reform Act Bundesgestzblatt I 2004/19. Schwaighofer, K. 2008. *Die neue Strafprozessordnung*, 17–32. Wien: Wiener Universitätsverlag. Koenig, F. A. and C. Pilnacek. 2008. 'Das neue Strafverfahren – Überblick und Begriffe'. *Österreichische Juristen-Zeitung* 10–17: 56–63.
12. Bertel, C. and A. Venier. 2014. *Strafprozessrecht*, 67–68. Wien: Manz Verlag. Fabrizy, E. E. 2014. *Strafprozessordnung*, 62–63. Wien: Manz Verlag.
13. Because there are no separate conviction and sentencing stages, judges are required to consider both together, using all relevant evidence. Murschetz, V. 2012. Child witnesses in Austria. In *Children and Cross-Examination – Time to Change the Rules?* ed. J. R. Spencer and M. E. Lamb, 133. Oxford: Hart Publishing Ltd.

14. The defence has a general right to access the case dossier and may request that further statements be added and that additional matters be investigated (Fabrizy, E. E. 2014. *Strafprozessordnung*, 129–132. Wien: Manz Verlag). The right to access can be limited, though, when ongoing investigations would be endangered by access.
15. Again, the importance of the dossier has to be mentioned. It stems from the fact that it is used by the trial judge to prepare for the trial and during the trial as well. Even though all the evidence, meaning all the statements and information, should be orally presented at the trial as well, the judge will always keep in mind what the witnesses and the accused have stated to the police in the investigative phase (Bertel, C. and A. Venier. 2014. *Strafprozessrecht*, 19. Wien: Manz Verlag).
16. Kirchbacher, K. 2009. '§ 252 StPO'. In *Wiener Kommentar zur Strafprozessordnung*, ed. H. Fuchs and E. Ratz, 5. Wien: Manz Verlag; Bertel, C. and A. Venier. 2014. *Strafprozessrecht*, 20–22. Wien: Manz Verlag.
17. Murschetz, V. 2015. Reform der Hauptverhandlung – adversatorische versus inquisitorische Hauptverhandlung. In *13. Österreichsicher StrafverteidigerInnentag*, ed. R. Soyer. Wien: NWV – neuer Wissenschaftlicher Verlag.
18. Murschetz, V. 2012. Child witnesses in Austria. In *Children and Cross-Examination – Time to Change the Rules?* ed J. R. Spencer and M. E. Lamb, 136. Oxford: Hart Publishing Ltd.
19. Murschetz, V. 2015. Reform der Hauptverhandlung – adversatorische versus inquisitorische Hauptverhandlung. In *13. Österreichsicher StrafverteidigerInnentag*, ed. R. Soyer. Wien: NWV – neuer Wissenschaftlicher Verlag. Schünemann, B. 2010 (2011). Reformaspekte des strafrechtlichen Haupt- und Rechtsmittelverfahrens. In *Die Reform des Haupt- und Rechtsmittelverfahrens*, ed. BMfJ, 9 (14 ff). Wien: NWV – neuer Wissenschaftlicher Verlag. Grande, E. 2000. Italian criminal justice: Borrowing and resistance. *The American Journal of Comparative Law* 48: 229.
20. Taylor, R. F. 1996. A comparative study of expert testimony in France and the United States: Philosophical underpinnings, history, practice and procedure. *Texas International Law Journal* 131 & 138.
21. Seiler, S. 2015. *Strafprozessrecht*, 35. Wien: Facultas Verlags-und Buchhandels AG. Bertel, C. and A. Venier. 2014. *Strafprozessrecht*, 20–21. Wien: Manz Verlag.
22. Seiler, S. 2015. *Strafprozessrecht*, 428. Wien: Facultas Verlags- und Buchhandels AG.
23. § 125 Code of Criminal Procedure.
24. See supra Section 2.2.
25. Taylor, R. F. 1996. A comparative study of expert testimony in France and the United States: Philosophical underpinnings, history, practice and procedure. *Texas International Law Journal* 131.
26. Schwaighofer, K. 2014. *Der Sachverständigenbeweis im Strafverfahren*, 15. Wien: Manz Verlag.
27. Schwaighofer, K. 2014. *Der Sachverständigenbeweis im Strafverfahren*, 4. Wien: Manz Verlag. Sumerauer, A. 2012. Die Stellung des Sachverständigen im Ermittlungsverfahren. In *Sachverständige in Österreich*: Festschrift 100 Jahre Hauptverband der Gerichtssachverständigen, ed. M. Rant, 307–315. Wien: Hauptverband der allgemein beeideten und gerichtlich zertifizierten Sachverständigen Österreichs.

28. Schwaighofer, K. 2014. *Der Sachverständigenbeweis im Strafverfahren*, 5. Wien: Manz Verlag.
29. § 2 Code of Experts and Interpreters; Bundesgesetz über die allgemein beeideten und gerichtlich zertifizierten Sachverständigen und Dolmetscher (SDG), BGBl 1979/137.
30. Todor-Kostic, A. 2011. Sachverständigenbeweis und Sachverständigenauswahl – Problembereiche im Lichte des § 126 StPO neu. *Anwaltsblatt*, 134.
31. Sumerauer, A. 2012. Die Stellung des Sachverständigen im Ermittlungsverfahren. In *Sachverständige in Österreich*: Festschrift 100 Jahre Hauptverband der Gerichtssachverständigen, ed. M. Rant, 307–315. Wien: Hauptverband der allgemein beeideten und gerichtlich zertifizierten Sachverständigen Österreichs. Todor-Kostic, A. 2011. Sachverständigenbeweis und Sachverständigenauswahl – Problembereiche im Lichte des § 126 StPO neu. *Anwaltsblatt*, 134.
32. § 126 Abs 4 Code of Criminal Procedure.
33. Bundesgesetz über die allgemein beeideten und gerichtlich zertifizierten Sachverständigen und Dolmetscher, BGBl 1979/137.
34. http://www.sdgliste.justiz.gv.at/.
35. Questioning the objectivity of experts assigned on a regular basis: Todor-Kostic, A. 2011. Sachverständigenbeweis und Sachverständigenauswahl – Problembereiche im Lichte des § 126 StPO neu. *Anwaltsblatt*, 133.
36. § 126 Abs 4 and 3 47 Abs 1 Code of Criminal Procedure. The expert is not impartial if he or she or a relative is the accused, a plaintiff in the combined civil suit, a representative in one of these instances or could have been caused harm by the conduct being prosecuted.
37. § 126 Abs 4 Code of Criminal Procedure.
38. Schwaighofer, K. 2014. *Der Sachverständigenbeweis im Strafverfahren*, 19. Wien: Manz Verlag. Pürstl, W. 2012. Generalprokuratur: Rechtswahrer der Republik im Strafrecht – Glaubwürdigkeitsgutachten: Welchen Stellenwert haben Privatgutachten. In *Sachverständige in Österreich*: Festschrift 100 Jahre Hauptverband der Gerichtssachverständigen, ed. M. Rant, 297-FN 6. Wien: Hauptverband der allgemein beeideten und gerichtlich zertifizierten Sachverständigen Österreichs.

Forensic Science in U.S. Criminal Trials after *Melendez-Diaz*

10

JESSICA SMITH

Contents

10.1 Introduction

In America, no court decision, with the possible exception of *Daubert*,[1] has had greater impact on the use of forensic science in criminal cases than the U.S. Supreme Court's 2009 decision in *Melendez-Diaz v Massachusetts*.[2] In that case, the High Court held that a forensic report cannot be admitted at trial without the testimony of the analyst who prepared it. The court determined that admitting a forensic report without the testimony of the preparing analyst violates a defendant's confrontation clause rights, protected by the Sixth Amendment to the federal constitution. This decision, binding on all federal and state courts in the nation, shook the criminal justice system. Prior to *Melendez-Diaz*, forensic reports such as toxicology reports in impaired driving cases, DNA reports in rape cases and autopsy reports in homicide cases routinely were admitted without the presence of the analyst who prepared them. In some cases, it simply was too costly or inconvenient for the prosecutor to bring the analyst to court. In others – such as cold cases – doing so was impossible because the analyst was deceased and the evidence could not be re-tested because it was consumed in the original testing or had been corrupted in the intervening years. *Melendez-Diaz* ended that practice, holding that if the prosecution wants to introduce forensic evidence in court, the analyst has to testify. Public crime labs, already struggling with backlogs,[3] felt the effects of *Melendez-Diaz* immediately. When cases were called for trial, analysts had to shut down their testing equipment and head to court. Depending on the geographic size of the jurisdiction and the lab's location, this could take hours or days, exacerbating testing backlogs. In North Carolina, for example, the tenth most populous state in the nation, 'court/travel time' for state crime lab toxicologists increased 600% in the 6 months after *Melendez-Diaz*.[4] Court time for that lab's DNA scientists doubled between 2009 and 2011.[5] By fiscal year 2013–14, North Carolina's crime lab analysts spent 2835 hours – 70.9 forty-hour work weeks – travelling to and testifying in court as required by *Melendez-Diaz*.[6] Not surprisingly, legislators and court officials sought ways to mitigate the impact of *Melendez-Diaz*. This chapter begins with a brief discussion of *Melendez-Diaz* and then explores the main legislative and administrative responses designed to ameliorate the impact of that case on criminal prosecutions.

10.2 *Melendez-Diaz*: The Case That Changed the Rules

Melendez-Diaz came in a line of confrontation clause cases originating with the U.S. Supreme Court's 2004 decision in *Crawford v Washington*.[7] The Sixth Amendment's confrontation clause provides that 'in all criminal prosecutions the accused shall enjoy the right ... to be confronted with the witnesses against him'.[8] In *Crawford*, the court radically revamped the analysis that applies to confrontation clause objections. *Crawford* overruled the old reliability test for confrontation clause objections and set in place a new, stricter standard for admission of out-of-court statements by people who do not testify at trial. Under the old test, an unavailable witness's statement was admissible if it had an 'adequate "indicia of reliability"',[9] a relatively easy test to satisfy. *Crawford* overruled prior case law, concluding that although the ultimate goal of the confrontation clause is to ensure reliability of evidence, 'it is a procedural rather than a substantive guarantee'.[10] It continued: the confrontation clause 'commands, not that evidence be reliable, but that reliability be assessed in a particular manner: by testing in the crucible of cross-examination'.[11] *Crawford* went on to hold that testimonial statements by declarants who do not appear at trial may not be admitted unless the declarant is unavailable and the defendant had a prior opportunity to cross-examine the declarant. Although the prosecution sometimes can establish the witness's unavailability (for example, when he or she is deceased), unless the witness has testified against the defendant at a prior trial, it typically cannot show a prior opportunity to cross-examine. *Crawford* itself dealt with the admissibility of a statement by the suspect's wife, made at the police station after being read her *Miranda* rights. Holding that the statement was testimonial, the court overturned the defendant's conviction, finding that it was error to admit his wife's statement without having her testify at trial.

In *Melendez-Diaz*,[12] a drug prosecution, the court extended the new *Crawford* rule to forensic reports. Specifically, the court held to be testimonial a report stating that the substance at issue was cocaine. The court further held that the defendant's confrontation rights were violated when the report was admitted into evidence to prove that the substance was cocaine without a witness to testify to its contents. The court went on to state in dicta that chain of custody evidence is testimonial as well.[13]

A dissenting justice lamented that the court's holding 'swe[pt] away an accepted rule governing the admission of scientific evidence' that had been in place for almost 100 years.[14] *Melendez-Diaz*'s impact on the use of forensic science in criminal trials was profound. The requirement that the analyst testify in court subjected cases to dismissal when analysts could not appear,[15] increased the cost of prosecution,[16] and created uncertainty about how many of the analysts involved in the testing have to appear at trial[17] and about the government's ability to prosecute old cases where forensic evidence was critical to the proof but the analyst was deceased and the evidence no longer available for re-testing. Not surprisingly, governments and government officials began looking for 'work-arounds'.

10.3 Responses to *Melendez-Diaz*

One response to *Melendez-Diaz* would be to dramatically increase crime lab funding so that there are enough analysts to handle existing testing dockets and testify live at trial. In tight budget times this solution has not come to pass. Thus, legislators and court officials have looked for alternatives to mitigate the impact of *Melendez-Diaz* on criminal prosecutions. The subsections that follow discuss the most common responses.

10.3.1 Substitute Analysts

An early prosecution response to *Melendez-Diaz* in cases where the testing analyst was unavailable to testify was use of a substitute analyst. Under this approach, the prosecution would subpoena another analyst who had not participated in the testing at issue. After being qualified as an expert, the witness would read the non-testifying analyst's report into evidence. If the defence made a confrontation clause objection, the prosecution would respond: 'We put a witness on the stand. Cross-examine him!'

That approach was short-lived. Two years after *Melendez-Diaz*, the U.S. Supreme Court decided *Bullcoming v New Mexico*,[18] applying *Melendez-Diaz* and holding that the defendant's confrontation rights were violated in an impaired driving case when the state's witness read into evidence a forensic report prepared by a non-testifying analyst. In *Bullcoming*, the prosecutor's evidence included a forensic lab report certifying that the defendant's blood alcohol concentration was above the threshold for aggravated impaired driving. At trial, the prosecution did not call the analyst who signed the certification. Instead, it 'called another analyst who was familiar with the laboratory's testing procedures, but had neither participated in nor observed the test on [the defendant's] blood sample'.[19] That witness read the report into evidence. The court held that this procedure violated the defendant's confrontation rights.

After *Bullcoming*, the prosecution tried another approach: bringing in a forensic expert who would testify to an independent opinion based on the non-testifying analyst's report but not admitting into evidence that report. Although the constitutionality of this procedure was considered by the U.S. Supreme Court in *Williams v Illinois*,[20] the court's fractured decision provides little guidance on the constitutionality of this procedure. In *Williams* the defendant was charged with, among other things, sexual assault of victim L.J. After the incident, L.J. was taken to the emergency room, where a doctor performed a vaginal exam and took vaginal swabs. The swabs and other evidence were sent to the Illinois State Police (ISP) Crime Lab for testing and analysis. An ISP forensic scientist, Brian Hapack, confirmed the presence of semen in the swabs. Months later, the defendant was arrested on unrelated charges and a blood sample was drawn from him pursuant to a court order. State forensic analyst Karen Abbinanti extracted a DNA profile from the sample and entered it into the ISP Crime Lab database. Meanwhile, L.J.'s swabs from the earlier incident were sent to Cellmark Diagnostic Laboratory for DNA analysis. Cellmark returned the swabs to the ISP Crime Lab, having derived a DNA profile for the person whose semen was recovered from L.J. Sandra Lambatos, a forensic specialist at the ISP lab, matched the Cellmark profile to the profile produced from the defendant's blood sample. The police then conducted a lineup, and L.J. identified the defendant as her assailant.

At trial, the state offered three expert forensic witnesses. First, Hapack testified that he confirmed the presence of semen on the swabs taken from L.J. Second, Abbinanti testified that she developed a DNA profile from the blood sample drawn from the defendant after his arrest, which she entered into the state forensic database. Third, Lambatos explained the techniques used to generate DNA profiles from blood and semen and how profiles could be matched to an individual based on the person's unique genetic code. Lambatos stated that when comparing DNA profiles, it is a 'commonly accepted' practice within the scientific community for one DNA expert to rely on another DNA expert's records. Lambatos testified that Cellmark was an accredited lab and that the ISP lab routinely sent evidence samples to Cellmark for DNA testing to expedite the process and reduce lab backlog. The prosecutor then asked Lambatos, 'Did you compare the semen that had been identified by Brian Hapack from the vaginal swabs of [L.J.] to the male DNA profile that had been identified by Karen [Abbinanti] from the blood of [the defendant]?' Lambatos answered yes. She testified that, based on her own comparison of the two profiles, she 'concluded that [the defendant] cannot be excluded as a possible source of the semen identified in the vaginal swabs' and that the probability of the profile appearing in the general population was '1 in 8.7 quadrillion black, 1 in 390 quadrillion white, or 1 in 109 quadrillion Hispanic unrelated individuals'. Asked whether she would 'call this a match to [the defendant]', Lambatos answered affirmatively. The Cellmark report was not admitted into evidence, Lambatos did not quote or read from the report, nor did she identify it as the source of her opinions.

On cross-examination, Lambatos confirmed that she did not conduct or observe the testing on the swabs and that her testimony relied on the Cellmark-produced DNA profile. She testified that she trusted Cellmark to do reliable work because it was an accredited lab but admitted that she had not seen Cellmark's calibrations or work in connection with the analysis at issue. The defence moved to exclude Lambatos's testimony regarding the Cellmark testing, arguing it violated the confrontation clause. The objection was overruled, and the defendant was convicted.

On appeal, the U.S. Supreme Court affirmed the conviction. Justice Alito wrote the plurality opinion, which was joined by Chief Justice Roberts and Justices Kennedy and Breyer. The plurality determined that no confrontation clause violation occurred for two reasons. The court determined that the Cellmark report fell outside of the scope of the confrontation clause because it was not used for the truth of the matter asserted and because it was non-testimonial. Justice Thomas concurred in judgment only. He agreed that the report was non-testimonial but reached this conclusion through different reasoning. Thomas disagreed with the plurality's conclusion that the report was not used for the truth for the matter asserted. Justices Kagan, Scalia, Ginsburg and Sotomayor dissented.

Under U.S. law, when a fragmented court decides a case and no single rationale explaining the result gets five votes, the court's holding is 'viewed as that position taken by those members who concurred in the judgments on the narrowest grounds'.[21] However, given the plurality opinion and that of Justice Thomas (which together make up the five votes to affirm), this rule is impossible to apply; rather than being broader or narrower, the opinions are just different. As such, the decision is best read as resolving only the matter in question.[22] Thus, while *Williams*-style substitute analyst testimony might be viable, use of such a technique clearly involves significant litigation risk. Pending further guidance from the Supreme Court, litigants and policy makers have looked to other techniques.

10.3.2 Notice and Demand Statutes

Although *Melendez-Diaz* was a blow to the prosecution, it contained a silver lining. Specifically, it noted that states are free to adopt procedural rules governing the exercise of confrontation objections.[23] The court discussed 'notice and demand' statutes as one such procedure. In their simplest form, these statutes require the prosecution to give the defendant notice that it intends to introduce a testimonial forensic report at trial without the testimony of the preparer. The defendant then has a period of time in which to 'object to the admission of the evidence absent the analyst's appearance live at trial'.[24] The court went on to note that simple notice and demand statutes are constitutional.[25]

Latching on to this language, legislatures responded. For example, after *Melendez-Diaz* North Carolina amended and enacted several notice and demand statutes.[26] The lower courts have uniformly held simple notice and demand statutes to be constitutional.[27] While this approach seems to be on solid constitutional ground, it has a practical limitation: the defence can object. Because defendants have a constitutional right to confront the analyst, nothing can stop them from lodging objections every time the prosecution gives notice under the statute. Knowing the difficulties in bringing analysts to court, some defendants simply object as a matter of course, betting that the prosecution will not be able to procure the analyst for trial and perhaps forcing a dismissal or a favourable plea offer. Thus, while on strong constitutional footing, this procedure has had limited practical impact.

10.3.3 Remote Testimony

Melendez-Diaz prompted renewed interest in remote testimony as a method to satisfy the confrontation clause. This procedure would allow analysts to testify from their labs or other close-by locations rather than travelling to court to do so. While such a procedure has the potential to significantly ameliorate the impact of *Melendez-Diaz* on crime labs,[28] it presents thorny constitutional issues.

The U.S. Supreme Court has decided two cases dealing with a criminal defendant's constitutional right to confront his or her accusers face-to-face. First, in *Coy v Iowa*,[29] the court held that a criminal defendant's confrontation rights were violated when two minor sexual assault victims testified behind a screen. The screen allowed the defendant 'dimly to perceive the witnesses', but the witnesses could not see the defendant at all.[30] After the defendant was convicted, he appealed, arguing that use of the screen violated his confrontation rights. The court agreed, finding it 'difficult to imagine a more obvious or damaging violation of the defendant's right to a face-to-face encounter'.[31] *Coy* thus established the rule that the confrontation clause protects the right to face-to-face confrontation.[32] This is understood to mean that the witness testifies live at trial, where the defendant and the witness can see and hear each other.

In 1990 – just 2 years later – the U.S. Supreme Court decided *Maryland v Craig*,[33] carving out an exception to *Coy*'s general rule. In *Craig*, the court upheld a Maryland statute that allowed a judge to receive, through a one-way closed-circuit television system, the testimony of an alleged child abuse victim. Under the system, the child witness, prosecutor and defence counsel went to a separate room while the judge, jury and defendant remained in the courtroom. The child witness was examined and cross-examined in the separate room, while a video monitor recorded and displayed the child's testimony to those in the courtroom. The procedure prevented the child from seeing the defendant as he or she testified. However, the child witness had to be competent to testify and to testify under oath; the defendant retained full opportunity for contemporaneous cross-examination, and the judge, jury and defendant were able to view by video monitor the demeanor of the witness as he or she testified. Throughout the procedure, the defendant remained in electronic communication with defence counsel, and objections were made and ruled on as if the witness were testifying in the courtroom. Upholding the procedure, *Craig* reaffirmed the importance of face-to-face confrontation of witnesses appearing at trial but concluded that such confrontation was not an indispensable element of the right to confront one's accusers. It held that while 'the Confrontation Clause reflects a *preference* for face-to-face confrontation … that [preference] must occasionally give way to considerations of public policy and the necessities of the case'.[34] It went on to explain that 'a defendant's right to confront accusatory witnesses may be satisfied absent a physical, face-to-face confrontation at trial only where denial of such confrontation is necessary to further an important public policy and only where the reliability of the testimony is otherwise assured'.[35]

As to the important public policy, the court found that 'a State's interest in the physical and psychological well-being of child abuse victims may be sufficiently important to outweigh, at least in some cases, a defendant's right to face his or her accusers in court'.[36] However, the court clarified that the state must make a case-specific showing of necessity. The court also noted that in the case before it, the reliability of the testimony was otherwise assured. Although the Maryland procedure prevented a child witness from seeing the defendant as he or she testified at trial, it required that the child be competent and testify under oath; the defendant had full opportunity for contemporaneous cross-examination; and the judge, jury and defendant were able to view the witness's demeanor while he or she testified.[37]

The U.S. Supreme Court has not yet decided whether *Craig* survives *Crawford* and if so, whether it is the appropriate analysis to apply to *two-way* remote testimony by child or other witnesses.[38] However, even before the court adopted its stricter confrontation clause analysis in *Crawford*, it expressed concern that the use of two-way video testimony beyond the *Craig* context would violate the confrontation clause. In 2002 – after *Craig* but before *Crawford* – the U.S. Judicial Conference submitted to the court a proposed change to the Federal Rules of Criminal Procedure that would have allowed for the use of remote testimony in federal criminal trials. The court rejected the proposed change, with Justice Scalia – who later authored the opinions in *Crawford* and *Melendez-Diaz* – expressing concern that it violated the confrontation clause.[39] As he put it, the issue is whether a criminal defendant 'can be compelled to hazard his life, liberty, or property in a criminal teletrial'.[40] Scalia answered this question in the negative, concluding: 'Virtual confrontation might be sufficient to protect virtual confrontation rights; I doubt whether it is sufficient to protect real ones'.[41] As to the distinction between one-way testimony (used in *Craig*) and the two-way testimony included in the proposed rule change, Scalia stated:

> I cannot comprehend how one-way transmission (which *Craig* says does not ordinarily satisfy confrontation requirements) becomes transformed into full-fledged confrontation when reciprocal transmission is added. As we made clear in *Craig*, a purpose of the Confrontation Clause is ordinarily to compel accusers to make their accusations *in the defendant's presence* – which is not equivalent to making them in a room that contains a television set beaming electrons that portray a defendant's image.[42]

Two justices dissented from the decision not to pass the proposed amendment on to Congress, arguing that it was constitutional under *Craig*.[43]

Other signals from the High Court suggest that *Craig*'s analysis for one-way testimony by child abuse victims may not apply to two-way testimony in other contexts. Consider the court's denial of review in *Wrotten v New York*,[44] a case that presented an opportunity for it to rule on the constitutionality of two-way systems under *Crawford*. In *Wrotten*, the victim, who was elderly, in poor health and unable to travel to court, was allowed to testify by way of live, two-way video. The defendant was convicted and the state's highest court upheld the conviction. Agreeing with the court's decision to deny review, Justice Sotomayor wrote separately noting that the issue was important and 'not obviously answered' by *Craig*.[45] She clarified that because the use of video testimony 'arose in a strikingly different context than in *Craig*, it is not clear that the latter is controlling'.[46]

The rejection of the proposed rule change and the commentary accompanying the denial of certiorari in *Wrotten* suggest that some members of the court question whether *Craig* survives *Crawford* and if it does, whether it governs two-way remote testimony by child or other witnesses. Notwithstanding this, many lower courts have ruled on the issue post-*Crawford* and have held that *Craig* applies to two-way video testimony.[47] But such rulings should not be interpreted as a green light to remote testimony by forensic scientists. Assuming that such a procedure can meet *Craig*'s requirement that reliability is otherwise assured, *Craig* still requires a showing of an important public policy interest. In *Craig* that interest was protecting child sexual assault victims. Other public policy interests that have been held to be equivalent and supporting the use of *Craig* procedures include protecting child witnesses,[48] national security,[49] combating international drug smuggling[50] and protecting critically ill witnesses[51] and witnesses who have been intimidated.[52] However, courts have either held or suggested that convenience,[53] mere unavailability,[54] cost savings[55] and general law enforcement[56] are insufficient to justify abridging a defendant's confrontation rights. These cases suggest that even if *Craig* survives *Crawford*, allowing two-way testimony by analysts to ease the state's administrative burden or lessen the cost of a trial will not pass constitutional muster.

There is, however, an approach to remote testimony that avoids these thorny legal issues. As noted above, the Supreme Court has endorsed the use of notice and demand statutes to procure valid waivers of confrontation rights. Some jurisdictions have skirted the constitutional issues regarding remote testimony by allowing the procedure only after a valid waiver is obtained through a notice and demand statute.[57] However, two practical limitations may impede widespread use of remote testimony in this manner: the up-front cost of equipping the courtroom and the remote location with the necessary technology and the fact that as with any notice and demand procedure, the defendant can object. And if the defendant objects, the analyst will be required to testify live at trial.

10.3.4 Pre-Trial Depositions

Under *Crawford*, testimonial statements by witnesses who do not testify at trial may not be admitted unless the state establishes unavailability and a prior opportunity to cross-examine. If a pre-trial deposition procedure can be developed to meet the constitutional standard for a prior opportunity to cross-examine, pre-trial deposition testimony would be admissible under *Crawford* when the witness is unavailable. Such a procedure likely would require the defendant's presence at the deposition, a requirement that will pose significant logistical and financial issues when the defendant is in custody pending trial. But when the defendant has been present at the deposition and the witness later becomes unavailable, several courts have upheld the use of pre-trial deposition testimony.[58]

Although such a procedure appears promising, it is unlikely to have much impact on testimony by lab analysts. Under *Crawford*, testimonial statements by witnesses who do not testify at trial may not be admitted unless the prosecution can establish unavailability and a prior opportunity to cross-examine. Even if a pre-trial deposition constitutes a prior opportunity to cross-examine, the prosecution still must establish the witness's unavailability for his or her testimonial statements to be admissible under *Crawford*.[59] The fact that a witness has died, for example, will satisfy this requirement. However, it is unlikely that mere inconvenience or cost to the prosecution will satisfy the constitutional requirement of unavailability.

10.3.5 Outsourcing Testing to Private Labs

With pressure mounting to deal with testing backlogs, interest has grown in the use of private labs and hospitals to perform forensic testing.[60] Supporters of this approach suggest that private labs are faster and cheaper than public labs.[61] Depending on the jurisdiction, private labs may offer advantages or disadvantages with respect to lab accreditation and certification of scientists. In any event, any such arrangements must address chain of custody and availability of private analysts to attend trial.

10.3.6 Imposing Fees for Analysts' Testimony

Another response to *Melendez-Diaz* has been legislation imposing fees on defendants when forensic analysts testify at trial.[62] Supporters of these statutes argue that they simply seek to provide funding needed for labs to comply with *Melendez-Diaz*. Critics, citing *United States v Jackson*,[63] say that they unconstitutionally chill confrontation rights. In *Jackson*, the Supreme Court held that if a 'provision ha[s] no other purpose or effect than to chill the assertion of constitutional rights by penalizing those who choose to exercise them, then it would be patently unconstitutional'.[64] It explained that if the statute has a legitimate government objective, that objective cannot be pursued 'by means that needlessly chill the exercise of basic constitutional rights'.[65] In the latter context, the question is whether the chilling effect is 'unnecessary and therefore excessive'.[66] However, the court has declined to adopt a broad reading of *Jackson*. In *Chaffin v Stynchcombe*,[67] for example, it noted that '*Jackson* did not hold … that the Constitution forbids every government-imposed choice in the criminal process that has the effect of discouraging the exercise of constitutional rights'.[68]

There do not appear to be any cases addressing '*Jackson* arguments' as to the new forensic fee statutes. However, many jurisdictions have general cost recoupment statutes that provide for recovery of 'reasonable costs of prosecution', and have been interpreted to allow for, among other things, the cost of testimony by government witnesses.[69] In the main, *Jackson* arguments have not succeeded as to these statutes.[70] The new forensic fee statutes are clearly distinguishable from general cost recoupment statutes and arguments can be made both ways about their constitutionality. But at this point, lawmakers and litigants will have to await court decisions for an answer.

10.3.7 Administrative Solutions

In geographically large jurisdictions, full-service regional labs can cut down on analysts' travel time in connection with testifying in court. Of course opening new labs requires new funding, which may not be available. Efficiency gains also can be achieved through administrative improvements designed to reduce unnecessary travel and wait time for analysts who are required to appear in court. These solutions include better communication between the prosecutor and the crime lab and procedures for the trial judge to streamline criminal cases involving forensic experts.[71]

10.4 The Future of Forensic Science in U.S. Criminal Trials

Notwithstanding the various attempts to ameliorate the impact of *Melendez-Diaz*, the case dramatically has increased the costs of criminal prosecutions involving forensic science, and has created pressure on the system in other ways. Lab delays have extended time to trial. The United States has high rates of pre-trial incarceration, including wealth-based detentions. Trial delays only exacerbate this issue, further fueling calls for reform of states' pre-trial systems.[72] Meanwhile, new reports have called some forensic disciplines into question.[73] Some prosecutors are responding by re-evaluating the routine use of forensic evidence, opting to use it only where absolutely necessary to secure a conviction. In light of these pressures, it is not unreasonable to think that lawmakers appropriating funds might begin to demand empirical evidence showing the cost–benefit of using forensic science in various categories of cases. Although hard to believe, the dramatic increased demand for forensic testing in the United States has not been accompanied by research showing the effectiveness of forensic evidence over other forms of evidence.[74] Such research might prove to be the most significant response to *Melendez-Diaz*. If that research controls for cultural and procedural differences, it could inform the use of forensic science in UK criminal trials as well.

Notes

1. *Daubert v Merrell Dow Pharmaceuticals, Inc.*, 509 U.S. 579 (1993) (seminal case setting out the standard of admissibility for expert testimony).
2. 557 U.S. 305 (2009).

3. See, e.g., Greg W. Steadman, U.S. Department of Justice, Bureau of Justice Statistics, Survey of DNA Crime Laboratories, 2001, 2 (2002), available at http://www.bjs.gov/content/pub/pdf/sdnacl01.pdf (backlogs at public DNA labs increased 135% between 1997 and 2000).
4. N.C. Department of Justice, North Carolina State Crime Laboratory Annual Report Fiscal Year 2013–14 (2014).
5. Id.
6. Id.
7. 541 U.S. 36 (2004).
8. U.S. Constitution Amendment VI.
9. *Crawford*, 541 U.S. at 40 (quoting *Ohio v Roberts*, 448 U.S. 56 [1980]).
10. Id. at 61.
11. Id.
12. 557 U.S. 305 (2009).
13. Id. at 311 n.1.
14. Id. at 330 (Kennedy, J., dissenting).
15. Id. at 340–41.
16. See, e.g., *Commonwealth v Musser*, 82 Va. Cir. 265, *4 (Va. Cir. Ct. 2011) (unpublished) (having the medical examiner testify at trial could cost $5000 or more); see also *Melendez-Diaz*, 557 U.S. at 341 (Kennedy, J., dissenting) (predicting that decision would impose 'enormous costs on the administration of justice').
17. *Melendez-Diaz*, 557 U.S. at 332–34 (Kennedy, J., dissenting).
18. 564 U.S. 647, 131 S. Ct. 2705 (2011).
19. Id. at 651, 131 S. Ct. at 2710.
20. 567 U.S. 50, 132 S. Ct. 2221 (2012).
21. *Marks v United States*, 430 U.S. 188, 193 (1977) (quotation omitted).
22. See, e.g., *People v Lopez*, 286 P.3d 469, 483 (Cal. 2012) (Liu, J., dissenting) ('The United States Supreme Court's most recent decision in this area produced no authoritative guidance beyond the result reached on the particular facts of that case'), cert. denied, 133 S. Ct. 1501 (2013).
23. *Melendez-Diaz v Massachusetts*, 557 U.S. 305, 314 n.3 (2009).
24. Id. at 326–27.
25. Id. at 327 n.12.
26. N.C. S.L. 2009-473 (N.C. sessions laws are available online, http://www.ncga.state.nc.us).
27. See, e.g., *State v Steele*, 689 S.E.2d 155, 161 (N.C. Ct. App. 2010).
28. Of the reported 2835 hours required by North Carolina State Crime Lab scientists to comply with *Melendez-Diaz*, only 9.7% of that time was spent testifying; the remaining hours are attributed to travel and time spent waiting to testify. North Carolina Department of Justice, supra note 3.
29. 487 U.S. 1012, 1016–22 (1988).
30. Id. at 1014.
31. Id. at 1020.
32. See id. at 1016.
33. 497 U.S. 836 (1990).
34. Id. at 849 (citations and internal quotation marks omitted).
35. Id. at 850.

36. Id. at 853.
37. Id. at 851.
38. *Horn v Quarterman*, 508 F.3d 306, 319 (5th Cir. 2007) (so stating); *Commonwealth v Musser*, 82 Va. Cir. 265 (Va. Cir. Ct. 2011) (unpublished) (same).
39. See Amendments to Rule 26(b) of the Federal Rules of Criminal Procedure, 207 F.R.D. 89, 93 (2002) (statement of J. Scalia).
40. Id. at 95 (emphasis omitted).
41. Id. at 94.
42. Id. (citations omitted).
43. Id. at 96–98 (dissenting statement of J. Breyer).
44. 560 U.S. 959 (2010).
45. Id.
46. Id.
47. Federal decisions include *United States v Abu Ali*, 528 F.3d 210, 238–43 (4th Cir. 2008); *United States v Bordeaux*, 400 F.3d 548, 554–55 (8th Cir. 2005); *United States v Yates*, 438 F.3d 1307, 1313 (11th. Cir. 2006); *United States v Fee*, 491 F. App'x 151, 158–59 (11th Cir. 2012) (No. 11-15356) (unpublished); *United States v Fee*, 425 F. App'x 847, 850 (11th Cir. 2011) (No. 09-15343) (unpublished); *United States v Prokop*, No. 2:09-cr-00022-MMD-GWF, 2014 WL 1154164 (D. Nev. Mar. 20, 2014) (unpublished); *United States v Sapse*, No. 2:10-CR-00370-KJD, 2012 WL 5334630, *2 (D. Nev. Oct. 26, 2012) (unpublished); *United States v Rosenau*, 870 F. Supp. 2d 1109, 1112–14 (W.D. Wash. 2012).

    State decisions include *State v Rogerson*, 855 N.W.2d 495 (Iowa 2014); *State v Stock*, 256 P.3d 899, 903–04 (Mont. 2011); *People v Buie*, 775 N.W.2d 817, 825 (Mich. 2009); *State v Seelig*, 738 S.E.2d 427, 434 (N.C. Ct. App. 2013); *Commonwealth v Musser*, 82 Va. Cir. 265 (Va. Cir. Ct. 2011) (unpublished); *State v Smith*, 308 P.3d 135, 136 (N.M. Ct. App. 2013); *People v Lujan*, 150 Cal. Rptr. 3d 727, 731 (Cal. Ct. App. 2012).
48. *Lujan*, 150 Cal. Rptr. 3d at 731–32; *State v Collins*, 65 So. 3d 271, 282 (La. Ct. App. 2011).
49. *Abu Ali*, 528 F.3d at 240–41 (al-Qaeda terrorism case).
50. *Rosenau*, 870 F. Supp. 2d at 1113.
51. *Bush v State*, 193 P.3d 203, 215 (Wyo. 2008); *Kramer v State*, 277 P.3d 88, 94 (Wyo. 2012); *Seelig*, 738 S.E.2d at 435; *People v Wrotten*, 923 N.E.2d 1099, 1103 (N.Y. 2009); *State v Sewell*, 595 N.W.2d 207, 211–13 (Minn. Ct. App. 1999); *Stevens v State*, 234 S.W.3d 748, 781 (Tex. App. 2007); *Paul v State*, 419 S.W.3d 446, 458–59 (Tex. App. 2012); *Sapse*, No. 2:10-CR-00370-KJD, 2012 WL 5334630 at *2.
52. *State v Johnson*, 958 N.E.2d 977, 989 (Ohio Ct. App. 2011).
53. *United States v Yates*, 438 F.3d 1307, 1316 (11th Cir. 2006) (en banc); *State v Smith*, 308 P.3d 135, 138–39 (N.M. Ct. App. 2013); *State v Rogerson*, 855 N.W. 2d 495, 507 (Iowa 2014); *Commonwealth v Musser*, 82 Va. Cir. 265 (Va. Cir. Ct. 2011) (unpublished); see also *Sapse*, No. 2:10-CR-00370-KJD, 2012 WL 5334630 at *2; *Rosenau*, 870 F. Supp. 2d at 1113.
54. *Rosenau*, 870 F. Supp. 2d at 1113 (stating that *Yates* requires more than convenience and unavailability and reasoning that in the case at hand there was real necessity where the witness was prevented from entering the United States as a result of a court order).

55. *Rogerson*, 855 N.W. 2d at 507; *Musser*, 82 Va. Cir. 265 ('The cost of protecting a constitutional right cannot justify its total denial' [quoting *Bounds v Smith*, 430 U.S. 817, 825 {1977}]); *United States v Prokop*, No. 2:09-cr-00022-MMD-GWF, 2014 WL 1154164, *2 (D. Nev. Mar. 20, 2014) (unpublished).
56. *United States v Abu Ali*, 528 F.3d 210, 241 (4th Cir. 2008).
57. See, e.g., N.C. Gen. Stat. § 15A-1225.3 and N.C. Gen. Stat. § 20-139.1(c)(5).
58. *United States v McGowan*, 590 F.3d 446, 456 (7th Cir. 2009); *United States v Smith*, 213 F. App'x 774, 776 (11th Cir. 2006) (unpublished); *State v Griffin*, 202 S.W.3d 670, 677 (Mo. Ct. App. 2006).
59. See, e.g., *United States v Tirado-Tirado*, 563 F.3d 117, 123–25 (5th Cir. 2009) (Mexican witness's videotaped pre-trial deposition improperly admitted where the government did not establish that the witness was unavailable); *State v Tribble*, 67 A.3d 210, 222 (Vt. 2012) (where the state's chief medical examiner was going to be out of the country at the time of trial, the court held that the medical examiner was not 'unavailable' despite the inconvenience and expense of international travel).
60. See, e.g., Steadman, supra note 2, at 1 (45% of surveyed public crime laboratories contracted with private laboratories to alleviate backlogs).
61. It is not entirely clear whether that is the case. See, e.g., N.C. Office of State Budget and Management, Cost Study of DNA Testing and Analysis 8 (2006) (showing that in-house DNA testing is less expensive than private lab testing).
62. See, e.g., N.C. Gen. Stat. § 7A-304(a)(11)–(12) (2013) (imposing $600 fee).
63. 390 U.S. 570 (1968).
64. Id. at 581.
65. Id. at 582.
66. Id.
67. 412 U.S. 17 (1973).
68. Id. at 30; see also *Fuller v Oregon*, 417 U.S. 40 (1974) (rejecting a *Jackson* claim); *Corbitt v New Jersey*, 439 U.S. 212, 218 (1978) ('cases … since *Jackson* have clearly established that not every burden on the exercise of a constitutional right, and not every pressure or encouragement to waive such a right, is invalid').
69. See, e.g., *People v Palomo*, 272 P.3d 1106, 1111 (Colo. App. 2011).
70. *United States v Palmer*, 809 F.2d 1504, 1506 (11th Cir. 1987); *United States v Wyman*, 724 F.2d 684, 688 (8th Cir. 1984); *United States v Chavez*, 627 F.2d 953, 955 (9th Cir. 1980); *United States v Fowler*, 794 F.2d 1446, 1449–50 (9th Cir. 1986); *United States v Escobar*, No. 87-0074-M, 1987 WL 31141, *5–6 (S.D. Cal. Sept. 30, 1987) (unpublished); *Com. v Coder*, 415 A.2d 406, 408 (Pa. 1980); *People v Estate of Scott*, 363 N.E.2d 823, 824 (Ill. 1977); *King v State*, 780 P.2d 943, 958 (Wyo. 1989); *State v Marinucci*, 321 N.W.2d 462, 467 (N.D. 1982).
71. Jessica Smith, Report on the NC State Crime Lab Working Group (Oct. 2014) (unpublished report) (copy on file with author) (setting forth 17 administrative recommendations to reduce forensic testing backlogs).
72. See generally, Jessica Smith, Bail Reform in North Carolina – Why the Interest? N.C. Crim. Law Blog (Feb. 14, 2019), https://nccriminallaw.sog.unc.edu/bail-reform-in-north-carolina-why-the-interest/.

73. President's Council of Advisors on Science and Technology, Forensic Science in Criminal Courts: Ensuring Scientific Validity of Feature-Comparison Methods (2016), https://obamawhitehouse.archives.gov/sites/default/files/microsites/ostp/PCAST/ pcast_forensic_science_report_final.pdf.
74. Joseph L. Peterson et al., Effect of Forensic Evidence on Criminal Justice Processing, 58 *J. Forensic Sci.* (Special Issue) S78 (Jan. 2013).

Index

N

O

P

R

S

Taylor & Francis Group
an informa business

For Product Safety Concerns and Information please contact our EU representative GPSR@taylorandfrancis.com
Taylor & Francis Verlag GmbH, Kaufingerstraße 24, 80331 München, Germany

www.ingramcontent.com/pod-product-compliance
Ingram Content Group UK Ltd.
Pitfield, Milton Keynes, MK11 3LW, UK
UKHW011016180926
475701UK00004B/780
9781498705691